SAILING

A BEGINNER'S GUIDE

Sailing is a wonderful sport and open to all. For the purposes of this book, we have had to use the terms 'helmsman' and 'he' throughout, but please interpret this as meaning either male or female.

SAILING

A BEGINNER'S GUIDE

The simplest way to learn to sail

TIM HORE

FERNHURST

BOOKS

First published in 2021 by Fernhurst Books Limited

The Windmill, Mill Lane, Harbury, Leamington Spa, Warwickshire. CV33 9HP, UK
Tel: +44 (0) 1926 337488 | www.fernhurstbooks.com
Copyright © 2021 Tim Hore

This book contains content previously published in Tim Hore's *Learn to Sail*, published by John Wiley & Sons Ltd.

A catalogue record for this book is available from the British Library
ISBN 978-1-912621-36-1

Cover photograph © Topper Sailboats
All other photos © Tim Hore / Fernhurst Books Limited

Designed & typeset by Daniel Stephen
Printed in Czech Republic by Finidr

CONTENTS

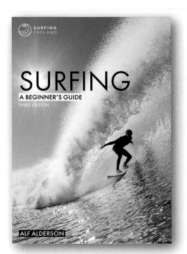
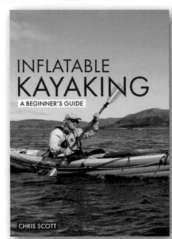
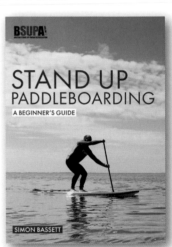

INTRODUCTION

Dinghy sailing is the most popular and best way to learn how to sail. It teaches you skills that can then be applied to yacht sailing, windsurfing or even kite surfing. With so many designs available, there is a dinghy to suit everyone's needs, from stable boats for beginners to high-performance machines for serious racers.

Sailing is a fantastic sport. Understanding where the wind is blowing from and realising how to harness this power is all absorbing and totally exhilarating. I have been a keen sailor since the age of 14, sailing dinghies, windsurfers and offshore yachts. I am a qualified RYA Senior Dinghy Instructor and regularly teach people of all ages to sail. My approach is always to help them enjoy the sport of sailing and my passion is for them to have fun.

Sailing: A Beginner's Guide is the perfect partner either for anyone new to dinghy sailing or for those looking to refresh their sailing techniques. Step-by-step instructions explain the basic skills of sailing a single- or two-person dinghy. You'll be guided through each stage of the learning process, starting with what you need to know prior to setting out on the water and how to stay safe.

Many of the photographs are taken from remote onboard cameras, including one at the top of the mast, to provide unique and highly instructive images. You can also go online to watch free video demonstrations showing you how to put the theory into practice – view them at www.fernhurstbooks.com: Search for *Sailing: A Beginner's Guide* and then click on 'Additional resources'. You can see full length instructional videos on our sailaboattv YouTube channel.

I hope you enjoy reading the book and, better still, become a keen sailor.

TIM HORE

KNOW YOUR BOAT

IN THIS CHAPTER YOU WILL LEARN THE TERMINOLOGY USED IN SAILING, AS WELL AS THE NAMES FOR THE PARTS OF YOUR BOAT, SAILS & RIGGING

THE BASICS
THE BOAT

Looking at a plan view of the hull, the left-hand side of the boat is called the **port** side and the right-hand side the **starboard** side. The front of the boat is called the **bow** and the rear is the **stern** or transom. Anything that happens ahead of the direction of travel is called **ahead**, and behind the boat is called **astern**.

The wind will push the boom to one side of the boat or the other – the side of the boat under the boom is called the **leeward** side, while the side of the boat opposite the boom is called the **windward** side. The leeward and windward sides of the boat will change, depending on the wind direction in relation to the boat's course (see the Points of Sailing chapter on page 37), but all the other descriptions mentioned above will always remain the same.

The helmsman holds the tiller and mainsheet in a dagger grip

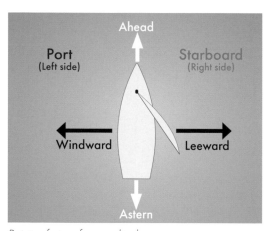

Points of view from a dinghy

The tiller extension is held in the back hand and the mainsheet in the front hand

THE SAILORS

The person steering the boat is called the **helmsman**, but when we use this term it applies to both male and female. The helmsman steers the boat by holding the **tiller extension** across and in front of his body with one hand, and the **mainsheet** in the other hand. This is called the dagger grip and allows him to control the **mainsail** and **rudder** easily.

In a two-person boat the second person is called the **crew**. This person controls the headsail called the **jib** and, if fitted, the **spinnaker**.

The second person is called the crew

Both the helm and the crew sit in an area called the **cockpit**, from where they operate the boat. To help them lean out and balance the boat, they can hook their feet underneath the **toestraps**, which are webbing straps securely fixed to the inside floor of the cockpit.

The helm and crew work as a team, they can use toestraps to lean out to balance the boat

DIFFERENT TYPES OF BOAT

Boats come in various shapes, sizes and construction to suit different crew weights, aspirations and sailing environments. The hull can be made from wood, fibreglass or hard-wearing durable plastic so, depending on what type of sailing you plan to do, there will always be an appropriate boat for you.

Rather than dashing out and buying the first boat you see, it is much better to try as many different types as possible to ensure that you purchase the best one for your needs. Sailing centres offer great advice and choice, while sailing clubs are also a good place for information and some even provide boats for hire.

For your first boat, perhaps consider a second-hand one – again your sailing centre or club can advise you on where to look.

Sailing has many levels... literally... is he sailing or flying?

BASIC COMPONENTS

Every boat has the same basic components, although variations apply from boat to boat. These components are the **hull** and **rudder assembly**, the **spars**, which consist of the **mast** and **boom** and are generally made of aluminium and finally the **sails**.

Two-person boats have two sails

Single-person boats are simpler in layout

To help with manoeuvring ashore you should use a **launching trolley**. The trolley supports the boat well when on shore and has large soft wheels that are designed to go in the water and make launching easier. The rope used to tie the boat to the trolley is called the **painter**. The painter can also be used when launching to tie the dinghy to a pontoon.

Launching trolleys make manoeuvring ashore easy

To tow your boat on the road you will need a **road trailer**. The launching trolley usually forms part of this configuration. You should avoid putting road trailers in the water as this can corrode the brakes and suspension.

THE HULL
BUOYANCY & DRAINAGE

Your boat should have at least two **buoyancy tanks** to keep you afloat. They are designed in such a way that, should one become holed, the boat will still float. The buoyancy tanks form the main body of the hull that you sit on, with an additional tank at the bow of the boat.

Boats have in-built buoyancy in the design

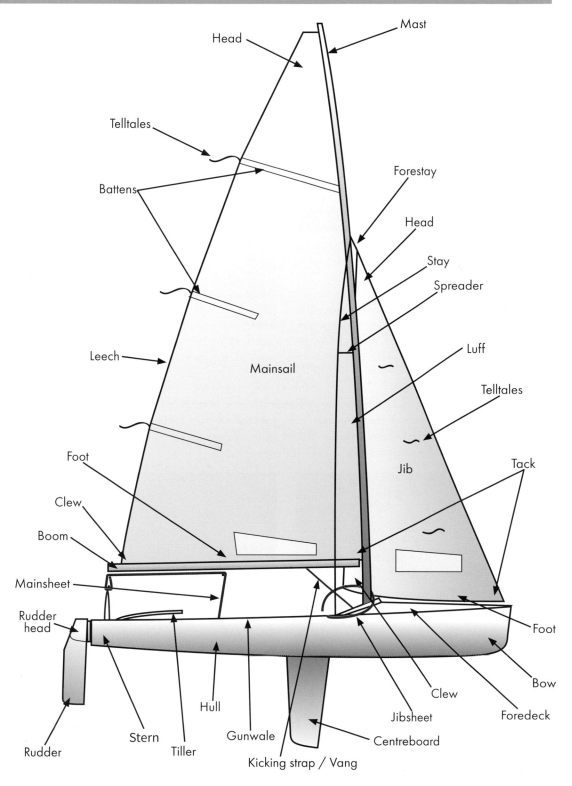

Head

Mast

Telltales

Forestay

Battens

Head

Stay

Spreader

Leech

Luff

Mainsail

Telltales

Foot

Jib

Tack

Clew

Boom

Mainsheet

Rudder head

Foot

Bow

Hull

Clew

Foredeck

Rudder

Stern

Tiller

Gunwale

Jibsheet

Centreboard

Kicking strap / Vang

A seat that runs sideways across the boat is called a **thwart**. The upper outside edge of the hull is called the **gunwale**.

Drainage holes are fitted at the back of the boat to allow you to drain any water that may collect in the buoyancy tanks while sailing. These holes are sealed with bungs, which must be fitted before you go afloat. The boat won't sink if you don't fit the bungs, but it will fill with water and be very difficult to steer.

Always check the bungs are fitted before going afloat

After sailing, when the boat is back ashore, raise the bow and remove the bungs to check for water draining out. If more than half a litre of water drains out, you should get the boat checked by a repair specialist as this indicates that there is a leak somewhere which should be fixed.

Some cockpits drain automatically when the boat is filled with water from either a capsize or near capsize. Boats that do not have an open stern or transom may be fitted with self-bailers. These are built into the hull and, when opened and pushed down, rely on the forward motion of the boat to drain the water out.

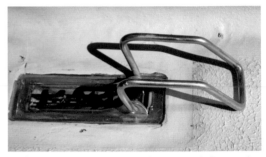

Self-bailers drain the boat when enough forward speed is maintained

CENTREBOARD

In the middle of the boat, you will have a **centreboard**, which either pivots and retracts around a pin, or slides up and down, in which case it is called a **daggerboard**. The centreboard is used to reduce the sideways force that the wind exerts on the sails and will therefore stop the boat slipping sideways. The Points of Sailing chapter on page 37 has more information on this.

Centreboards can pivot up...

... and down around a central pin

Or slide up...

... and down; if it is a daggerboard

RUDDER

At the stern of the boat is the rudder assembly. The **rudder blade** is your steering mechanism. Unlike a car that is steered by a wheel, dinghies have a rudder blade that works in the same way as the tail fin on an aircraft. With the rudder blade centrally positioned, the boat will sail in a straight line, but with even the smallest degree of angle on the rudder blade the boat will turn and continue to turn until the blade is central once more.

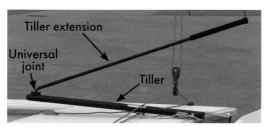

The tiller extension is held by the helmsman

The angle of the rudder blade is controlled by an arm attached to the rudder called the tiller. The helmsman holds the **tiller extension** which connects to the tiller via a universal joint.

The rudder blade is held in place with the **rudder stock** – this is a vertical post at the forward edge of the rudder, on which are a couple of fittings called **pintles**. These marry up with fittings on the transom, known as **gudgeons**, enabling the rudder to pivot easily.

The rudder blade usually lifts around a pin, which makes launching and recovering the boat from the water easier. Once lowered, the rudder blade is secured in place with a control line called the rudder downhaul, which is in turn secured with a small jam cleat on the tiller.

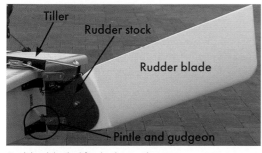

Rudder blade lifted when ashore

RIGGING

Rigging is the generic term given to the collection of wires and ropes that support a mast and sails.

There are two ways that the mast and sails are secured to the boat. On some boats like the Laser shown in the photograph, the mast is inserted into a pocket on the mainsail and the whole assembly lifted and set into a socket on the hull. In this configuration the mast is relatively unsupported but, due to the reasonably small sail, the load on the rig is somewhat limited.

Some boats have unsupported masts that slot into sockets on the deck

For larger boats where more load is introduced from the sails, wire rigging is used to support the **mast**. The side rigging consists of **shrouds**, with one each side of the hull, and the front wire is called a **forestay**. It is important to use all three wires to prevent the mast from bending or breaking whilst sailing. You may also have **spreaders** fitted on the mast. These are horizontal brackets that help to further spread the load of the sail to the mast.

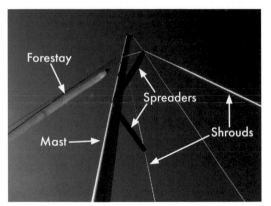

Most boats have wire rigging to support the mast and maybe spreaders

Boats with supporting rigging are fitted with rope or wire to hoist the sails. These lines are called **halyards** and are connected to the top of the sail. They are pulled to hoist the sail and then secured in place when the sail is fully up. They are simply then released to drop the sail back down again.

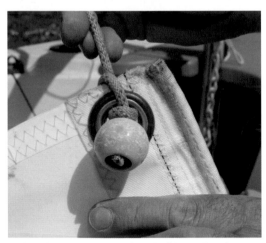

Halyards connect to the head of the sail and are used to hoist the sails

On a two-person boat it is now common to have a **furling system** for the jib. This simple system allows the rigged and hoisted sail (jib) to be rolled up and temporarily packed away without the need to fully lower the sail, for example during rigging and launching and even when learning to use the spinnaker. The control line to furl the jib is called the **furling line**.

A furling system can be fitted to the jib, here furled

Unfurling the sail is quick and easy to do

BOOM

The boom connects to the mast with a flexible joint called a **gooseneck**. This can be either loosely connected, slotting into the end of the boom, or it can be permanently fixed to the mast.

For a loose fitting gooseneck, the boom has a hole into which the gooseneck slides. It is held in place once the outhaul control line is pulled tight.

The end of the boom slots over a fitting on the mast called a gooseneck

Some boats have a permanently fixed gooseneck

TOP TIP

It is the design of the boat and rigging that dictates which gooseneck option your boat is fitted with. Loose fitted goosenecks tend to be on older designs of boat, with more modern boats utilising the fixed gooseneck.

BURGEE

To help identify where the wind is blowing from when sailing, you may also have a flag at the top of your mast. This is called a burgee and the tip points towards the wind. If you have one, keep an eye on it at all times to develop your wind awareness.

Masthead burgees indicate wind direction

SAILS

Single-person dinghies have one sail while two-person dinghies have two or sometimes three sails.

Single-person boats have one sail

KICKING STRAP / VANG

All boats should have a **kicking strap** or **vang**. This is a device that prevents the boom from rising up when the mainsail is released. Without the kicking strap, the boat will be extremely hard to control, particularly when the wind gets stronger.

The kicking strap has two possible configurations; one will push the boom down, and the other will pull it down – these configurations are purely down to boat design and both have the same effect on the mainsail.

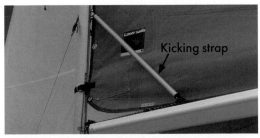

Kicking straps can push the boom down...

... or can pull the boom down; both systems have the same effect

Sail cloth is a man-made fabric that is reasonably hard wearing yet flexible enough to allow it to take the shape of a wing when set correctly. Air travelling at different speeds on each side of the sail generates lift, consequently driving the boat through the water.

The big sail (and only one on a single-person dinghy) is called the **mainsail**. A two-person boat will have an additional smaller sail at the front of the boat. This sail is called the **jib**.

Sails are generally triangular in shape with three corners and rigged with the narrow part of the triangle at the top.

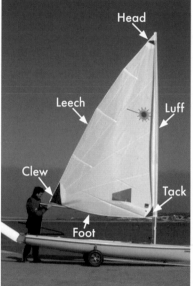

Most sails are triangular in shape – here a spinnaker, mainsail and jib

Regardless of which sail it is, the corners all have the same description. The top of the sail is called the **head**, the front bottom corner is called the **tack** and the other corner is called the **clew**. The leading edge of the sail is called the **luff**, the trailing edge is called the **leech**, and the bottom edge is called the **foot**.

MAINSAIL

To stop the leech of the mainsail from flapping while you are sailing, sail battens are inserted into pockets along its length.

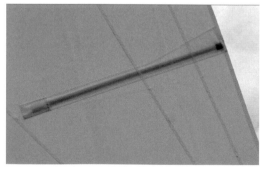

Sail battens usually inserted into the mainsail help the sail to hold its shape

At the tack of the mainsail the design of your boat will have one of two configurations for controlling the leading edge or luff of the sail.

On boats with a floating tack on the sail this is called a **downhaul**.

The downhaul pulls the front edge (luff) of the sail down

On boats where the tack of the sail is hard fixed to the end of the boom by the gooseneck, it is called a **cunningham**.

Both do the same job. As the wind increases, this control line should be pulled tighter, which depowers the sail slightly, making it easier to control. Conversely in light winds this control line should be kept quite loose.

Your mainsail may also have a **reefing system**. Reefing is the term given to the process of reducing the amount of mainsail area. For a full explanation read the Reefing chapter on page 169.

Alternative downhaul arrangement called a cunningham

SPINNAKER

Two-person boats may also be fitted with a spinnaker. This is a large sail made of a very lightweight cloth that can only be used when the boat is sailing across or away from the direction the wind is blowing from. This sail will introduce a whole new dimension of fun to your sailing and is launched from a chute, controlled by the crew and supported with a retractable bowsprit. (See the Asymmetric Spinnaker chapter on page 147 for a detailed explanation of this sail.)

TELLTALES

Telltales are small strips of fabric that are stuck on both sides of the sail and positioned towards the front edge or luff of the sail. These are there to help you when sail setting. When set correctly they stream horizontally; when the sail is set incorrectly, they flutter violently.

On single-person boats telltales are found on the leading edge of the mainsail, while on two-person boats they are mostly fitted to the jib.

Telltales will react before the sail flutters so the amount of sail control or course alteration required to set the telltales is often subtle. For more information on how to use telltales, see page 51.

Spinnaker sailing

Telltales help to identify how to set the sail

ROPES

Control sheets are used to pull the sails in and out

The ropes used to pull any sail in and out are called **sheets**. You will have a mainsheet to control the mainsail. The mainsheet will have a pulley system allowing the helmsman to adjust the mainsail easily when it is under load. The pulleys are either at the end of the boom or in the centre of the cockpit and are called the mainsheet falls.

In a two-person dinghy you will have a jibsheet to control the jib, and a spinnaker sheet to control the spinnaker.

Jibsheets control the jib

The mainsheet controls the mainsail; this can come in different configurations

All further ropes on board used to control other aspects of the sail or other fixtures are generically called control lines.

Sail control lines

These are held in place with fixtures called **fairleads**. A fairlead can either be a pulley or a non-moving captive fixing such as a ring or hook and is used to guide a rope as well as prevent it from chafing. Always tie a stopper knot in the end of all control lines to prevent them running free.

Pulleys fixed to the deck are called fairleads

Holding on to a fully powered sail can be hard work so to help with this a jam cleat can be used. Jam cleats come in different configurations, but all do the same thing: allowing you to lock a particular control line.

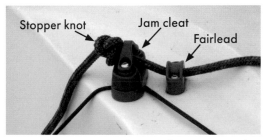

Stopper knot   Jam cleat   Fairlead

A jam cleat secures a sheet under tension and makes it easier to use; always tie a stopper knot in the end of the rope

The mainsheet can have its own jam cleat integrated in one unit with a pulley

Always hold the mainsheet so you can free the sail in the event of a gust

TOP TIP
The helmsman must always hold the mainsheet when sailing, even if it is held in place with the mainsheet jammer. He must be able to quickly release the sail in the event of a gust to prevent an unwelcome capsize.

RIGGING

RIGGING CAN BE COMPLICATED, SO IT IS IMPORTANT TO HAVE A CORRECT
UNDERSTANDING OF ALL THE COMPONENTS ON THE BOAT & HOW THEY FIT TOGETHER

As well as being a term to describe the structure above the boat (see page 15), rigging is also the general term used to describe the action of preparing the boat for sailing by attaching the sails and rudder.

As already mentioned, there are two main styles of rigging. The first is an unsupported mast where the mast is inserted into a pocket on the mainsail and the whole assembly is then lifted into a socket on the hull of the boat.

With an unsupported mast, the mainsail slides over the mast

And the entire rig is lifted into place

The other main style of rigging is the Bermuda style. This is where the mast is supported with a series of wires at the side and bow of the boat, and the sails are hoisted by control lines called halyards.

With a Bermuda rig, the mainsail is hoisted by a halyard

The process for hoisting the sails is basically the same, regardless of where you are launching. However, when launching from a beach, the mainsail is usually hoisted on the shore before the boat is put into the water, whereas when launching from a pontoon, the boat is tied to the pontoon before the mainsail is raised.

Rig the sail on the shore if you are launching from a beach

On a pontoon use the leeward side to attach the boat to rig it

TOP TIP

When rigging any sail ashore, if there is enough space, try to ensure that the bow of the boat is pointing towards the wind. This will stop the wind from catching the sail and blowing it into the mud.

Park the boat head to wind before hoisting the mainsail

For more information on this, read the Launching & Recovery chapters on pages 75 and 89.

BERMUDA RIG

On this rig, the mast is supported with two wires of equal length to either side called shrouds and one to the front called the forestay. The foot of the mast is stepped into a fixture on the hull or foredeck and the wire rigging is connected to fixed plates on the side and bow of the boat.

The sails are pulled up using halyards, which can be made from either a very strong non-stretch rope or a wire with a short rope tail. This is purely down to mast design and personal preference, and both do the same job.

On a two-person boat you will have two sails to rig; these are the mainsail and jib (we'll come onto the spinnaker later).

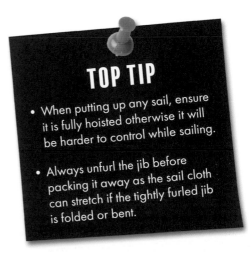

TOP TIP

• When putting up any sail, ensure it is fully hoisted otherwise it will be harder to control while sailing.

• Always unfurl the jib before packing it away as the sail cloth can stretch if the tightly furled jib is folded or bent.

Fully rigged two-person dinghy

RIGGING THE JIB

Remove the jib from its storage bag, unroll it, keeping the sail clear from contact with the ground, and place the sail on the foredeck. Then get hold of the jib halyard and check above to make sure it is not tangled in the rigging.

Next, connect the jib halyard to the top corner (head) of the sail with the shackle and split ring. Do not hoist the sail yet.

You then connect the front corner of the jib (tack) to the fitting on the bow with the shackle and split ring.

Pass one of the jibsheets through the fairleads on the deck of the boat – these should be near the shrouds – and thread the rope through the jam cleat, tying a figure-of-eight stopper knot (see page 164) in the end. This will prevent the rope from running free when sailing.

Repeat the process on the other side of the boat with the other jibsheet.

Next, hoist the jib, ensuring that the bow of the boat is pointing towards the wind. Pull on the jib halyard tail, keeping an eye on the sail to make sure it does not get tangled during the hoist.

To stop the sail falling on the ground and getting dirty, one person hoists the sail while the other guides it.

When the wire halyard comes out of the mast, connect this to the hook on the jib tension system, which is located nearby. Pull this tension system tight; you need to pull as hard as you can to make sure the rigging is taut.

A rough guide to checking the tension of the shrouds is to give them a pluck. Rigged tightly, the shrouds behave in the same way as a guitar string, and you should hear an audible 'twang'.

To stop the sail from flapping in the wind for the rest of the rigging and launching process, pull on the jib furling line, if you have one, to temporarily store the jib. This line is usually located under the foredeck near the mast.

Connect the head of the jib to the jib halyard

Tack of sail connected

Hoist the jib – one person pulls and the other steadies the sail

The rigging should be tight; when the shroud is plucked a low note should be heard

Attach the tack of the jib to the bow of the boat

Pass each jibsheet through its fairlead and tie a figure-of-eight knot on the end

Connect the halyard end to the tension system on the mast

Furl the jib

TOP TIP

The jib halyard must be pulled tight, otherwise the boat will not be able to head as close to the no-go zone as needed to allow you to successfully sail towards the wind. On boats that do not have a jib tension system, the crew can gently pull on the forestay once the jib is hoisted. This pulls the top of the mast forward and makes it easier to secure the halyard tightly.

RIGGING THE MAINSAIL

Position the boat with the bow pointing towards the wind.

Mainsails can be rigged either on a beach or on a pontoon. The process is the same, but it is vital that the bow of the boat is pointing directly into the wind before you attempt to do this:

- Take the sail out of its bag and place it in the boat, with the luff edge of the sail by the mast.
- The luff has a rope sewn into the sail to keep the sail secure in the mast track when the sail is hoisted.
- Unroll the sail loosely, ensuring the sail remains in the boat.
- Untie the mainsail halyard from where it is stored (usually tied to the shroud) and connect the halyard to the head of the sail. Here simply make a loop close to the end of the halyard and poke this loop through the eyelet on the sail.
- Bend the tail back and pass the plastic stopper back through the loop created.
- Pull the halyard tight to hold the stopper in place.
- Take the head of the sail and slide this into the track located on the back of the mast. Pull the slack out of the halyard.
- One person should pull the halyard to hoist the sail while the other person guides the sail into the track, making sure it does not jump free.

- Continue hoisting until the sail is fully raised, but note that the higher the sail goes, the harder you will need to pull. Look above to check the sail is fully hoisted.
- To keep the sail at the top of the mast, lock the halyard in the jam cleat, which should be located nearby.
- Tidy up the rest of the halyard and store it safely. Most boats have small bags fitted for this purpose.

TOP TIP

When connecting the halyard, first look above to check it isn't caught up around the shroud (see photo 6).

Some sails have an extra restraining strap near the tack of the sail. If you have this, loop it around the mast and secure it.

Next, secure the tack of the sail. This is controlled with a control line called the downhaul. Loop the downhaul through the eyelet on the sail and secure it back to the boom with either a bowline around the gooseneck or slide a small stopper knot in the mast track just below the gooseneck. For more information on knots, see the Knots chapter on page 163.

Pull the downhaul tight and secure it in the cleat on the side of the mast.

The next step is to rig the clew of the sail:

- The clew of the sail is inserted into a track on top of the boom and pulled out to the end.
- The outhaul line is then threaded through the eyelet on the sail and looped back to the end of the boom, with the end of the line secured to a point on the boom.
- Tighten the clew outhaul by pulling on the other end of this line, near the mast.
- Continue pulling the line tight until the sail is near the end of the boom. This keeps the sail flat, which will be easier to handle afloat.
- When the clew outhaul is correctly tensioned, the foot of the sail should have approximately 5cm of curve at the mid-point of the boom.

With the sail and boom now attached, the mainsheet is then simply threaded between the blocks on the boom and on the boat.

Poke the end of the mainsheet through the mainsheet jam cleat and tie a figure-of-eight stopper knot (see page 164) in the end of the rope to stop it running free when sailing.

TOP TIP

Try to buy a mainsheet of 7mm diameter as this is slightly thinner than most standard mainsheets (typically 8mm in diameter). The thinner rope will run through the blocks easier, allowing you to adjust the sail easier. Be aware that a rope of this thickness will be harder on the hands, so be sure to wear gloves.

Place the luff of the sail near the mast and unroll the sail

Locate and untie the halyard from the shroud

Make a loop in the end of the halyard and poke it through the head of sail

Bend the plastic stopper back and pass through the loop

Pull the halyard tight

Look above to ensure the halyard is not tangled

Feed the luff rope into the mast track and gently hoist

Look at the top of the mast to check the sail is fully hoisted

Lock the halyard in the cleat

Tidy up the halyard tail

Store the halyard tails

Wrap securing strap around the mast if there is one

Pull securing strap tight and lock it off

Pass the downhaul through the tack of the sail

Secure the downhaul back to the mast

Pull the downhaul tight

Secure the downhaul

Thread the outhaul line through the clew of the mainsail

Secure the end of the outhaul to the boom

Pull the clew outhaul tight...

... so the clew is close to the end of the boom

The sail should have c. 5cm of curve at the mid-point of the boom

Thread the mainsheet through the pulley assembly on the boom

Tie a figure-of-eight stopper knot in the end of the mainsheet

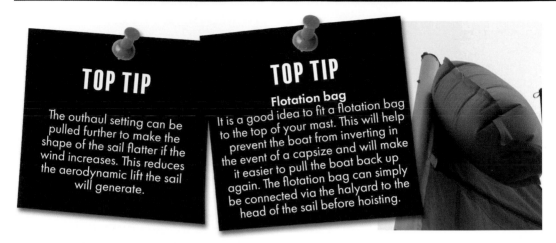

TOP TIP

The outhaul setting can be pulled further to make the shape of the sail flatter if the wind increases. This reduces the aerodynamic lift the sail will generate.

TOP TIP

Flotation bag
It is a good idea to fit a flotation bag to the top of your mast. This will help prevent the boat from inverting in the event of a capsize and will make it easier to pull the boat back up again. The flotation bag can simply be connected via the halyard to the head of the sail before hoisting.

ALTERNATIVE SET-UP FOR THE MAINSAIL

An alternative configuration is for the foot of the mainsail to slide along a track on top of the boom, with both ends secured prior to hoisting the sail.

The sail and boom are then hoisted as one item and the gooseneck slotted into place. In this configuration, the kicking strap usually works by pulling the boom down. For more information on kicking straps, see pages 17 and 54.

With the bow of the boat pointing towards the wind, hoist the sail to the top of the mast and secure the halyard in place. During the hoist, the wind will cause the boom to flap with the sail. This can result in injury or damage, so be careful to keep your head out of the way. Next, gently push down on the boom and slide the gooseneck into the end of the boom.

For boats of this type, the downhaul is called a cunningham. Simply thread the cunningham through the eyelet on the sail and secure it around the gooseneck with a bowline.

Some sails are close fitted to the boom with the foot of the sail slid along the track on the top of the boom

The gooseneck on the mast slots into the end of the boom

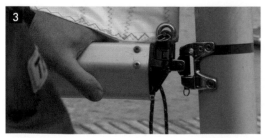

The gooseneck is now fully connected to boom

The cunningham control threads through a second eyelet just above the tack

WIRE HALYARDS

Your boat may be fitted with a wire main halyard. In this situation the shackle is fitted to the head of the mainsail, and when the sail is hoisted the end of the halyard fits over a rack at the bottom of the mast.

A wire halyard connects to the head of the sail with a shackle

Wire halyards have a rope tail that is pulled to hoist the sail. This halyard and tail each have a loop which are connected together. It is personal preference as to which one you opt for on your boat and it is possible to change from one to the other. Wire halyards offer more consistency as it is easier to spot when the sail is pulled to the top of the mast.

Loop the end of the wire halyard over the rack on the mast to secure it when the sail is hoisted

With any sail it is important to pull the sail fully up; in particular, the mainsail and spinnaker. When hoisted, look above to check that the sail is as far up as it can go.

Mainsails tend to have a black band painted on the tip of the mast. The mainsail should be pulled up to that point.

UNSTAYED MAST

Some single-person dinghies don't have wire rigging to support the mast. On these boats the sail has a permanent pocket in which the mast is inserted prior to lifting. The whole unit is then lifted and placed into the deck of the boat.

Mainsails on this type of mast do not have a track along the boom to hold the foot of the sail in place. The clew of the sail is connected to the outhaul on the boom, using the outhaul control line (this is looped through the sail and then attached to the end of the boom).

On a boat like a Laser, it is important to tie the clew down as well as out, otherwise it rides up, which makes the sail harder to handle when sailing. Special fixtures can be purchased for just this situation; however, as an alternative, thread a short piece of line through the clew of the sail and wrap this twice around the boom before tying both ends together with a reef knot (see page 165).

The clew outhaul will rise up if not restrained...

... so tie the clew down to the boom

SAIL BATTENS

Most mainsails have fibreglass battens that are inserted into the trailing edge or leech of the sail. These are designed to stop the leech flapping. Your mainsail may have three or more battens of different lengths and each are inserted into elasticated pockets that are built into the sail.

To check you have the right one, lay the batten on the surface of the sail. Note that, if there is one, the curved or thinner end of the batten is the end to be inserted first.

Once you have identified the correct batten for the pocket, push it into the sail. Keep pushing until you reach the end; then ease the batten so that it pops back into the sealed pocket on the sail.

Lay the batten on sail before inserting it into the pocket to make sure it is the right one

Insert the curved tip or thinner end of the batten into the pocket opening

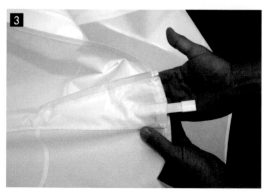

Continue pushing the batten in until the end of the pocket is reached

Push into the elasticated pocket

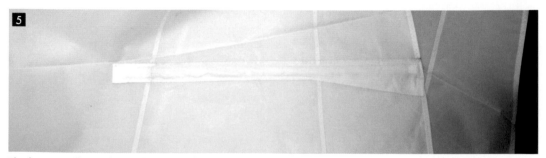

The batten will sit in the sealed part of the pocket

RUDDER

If you have a lifting rudder, fit it to the stern of the boat with the blade raised and make sure the safety clip is secured.

This prevents the rudder from falling off in the event of capsizing. For more details on the rudder assembly, refer to page 15.

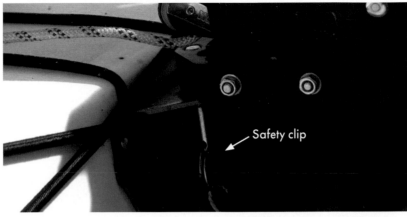

Ensure the safety clip is fixed to the rudder assembly

Safety clip

DE-RIGGING

This is basically the reverse of the rigging process. When the sails are lowered, be careful to keep them off the ground to stop them getting muddy.

Sails are either folded in a series of large flakes or rolled up from the head. This depends on the structure of the sail cloth and whether sail battens are left permanently in the sail. Try to dry any sails that are wet by hanging them in a suitably large place if you can.

For storage, return the sails to the sail bags and keep in a dry place.

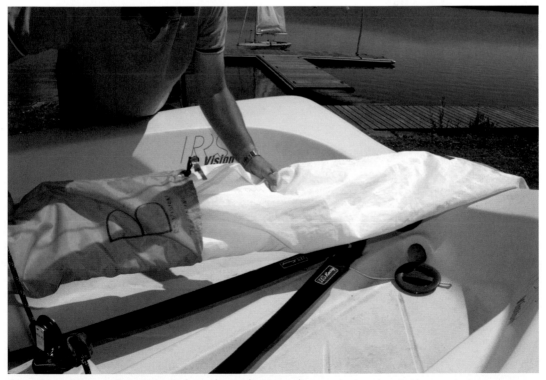

Store the sails in a sailbag to keep them clean when stored

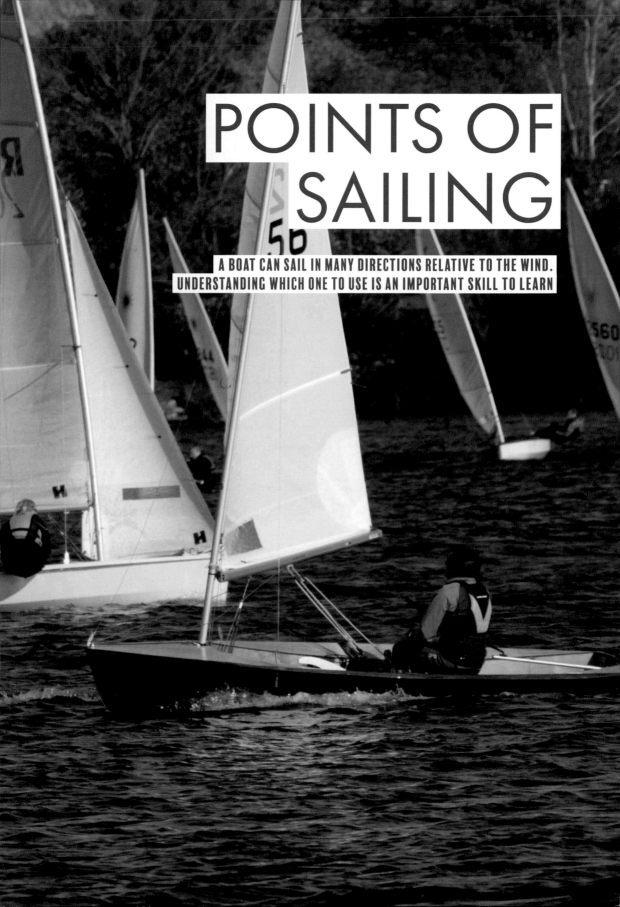

POINTS OF SAILING

A BOAT CAN SAIL IN MANY DIRECTIONS RELATIVE TO THE WIND. UNDERSTANDING WHICH ONE TO USE IS AN IMPORTANT SKILL TO LEARN

WHAT IS A POINT OF SAILING?

The term 'points of sailing' refers to each point that a boat can sail relative to where the wind is blowing from. This chapter will help you to understand what the different points of sailing are.

It is very important to be aware of where the wind is coming from at all times as this is fundamental to everything that you will do in the boat. Once you have learnt to easily identify the wind direction, understanding what to do with the sails will become second nature. The wind is the fuel that drives the boat and the sails are the engine that should be tuned for optimum performance.

To help you recognise where the wind is blowing from you can use a masthead burgee, if you have one, which will point towards the wind. Flags ashore are another indicator as they simply flutter in line with the wind, or ripples and waves on the water also move in the direction of the wind. Alternatively, when afloat, you can release the sails fully and they will flap like a flag, identifying the direction of the wind.

Flags ashore indicate wind direction

Ripples or waves on the water move in the same direction as the wind

A flapping sail acts like a flag and can be used to help identify where the wind is blowing from

Also bear in mind that the wind regularly changes direction (called windshifts), usually by no more than 10°. This is particularly noticeable when sailing on the close-hauled point of sailing.

Any point of sailing where the boat has the wind on its left-hand side is called sailing on port. Any point of sailing where the wind is blowing from the right-hand side is called sailing on starboard. Each point of sailing can be achieved on either port or starboard tack.

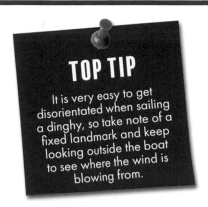

TOP TIP

It is very easy to get disorientated when sailing a dinghy, so take note of a fixed landmark and keep looking outside the boat to see where the wind is blowing from.

When the wind is on the left-hand side, the boat is on port tack

When the wind is on the right-hand side, the boat is on starboard tack

Remember that the boat will turn very quickly with even the smallest amount of rudder / tiller movement, and to optimise good performance the sails need to be either pulled in or released every time the course is changed.

To sail effectively you need to harness the power of the wind and adjust the settings of the sails and centreboard to suit the point of sailing you are on. It is vital to remember that as your boat turns even by a small amount, the point of sailing will alter. For more information on this read the Key Factors chapter on page 47.

HOW A SAIL WORKS

Harnessing the wind efficiently is important if you want to sail effectively. A sail works in the same way as an aircraft wing, with wind travelling across both sides of it. The wind on the leeward side of the boat, i.e. the side of the boom, opposite where you should be sitting, will be travelling faster than the wind on the windward side, i.e. the side you should be sitting on, closest to the wind. This imbalance of speed and pressure causes lift, which drives the boat through the water.

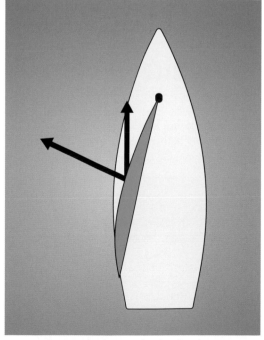

Air travelling on the leeward side of sail is compressed, which generates lift

NO-GO ZONE

Once you have identified where the wind is blowing from, the first point to appreciate is the area called the no-go zone. This is an area that is 45° either side of the line down which the wind is blowing. In the no-go zone the sails don't work. You should try to avoid accidentally sailing into this zone as the sails will mimic a flag and flap uncontrollably above your head, bringing your boat to a stop.

You can sail in any other direction (point of sailing) apart from straight into the wind, i.e. into the no-go zone. Your wind awareness will help you to keep a constant eye on where the no-go zone is.

Keep clear of the no-go zone as the sails don't work

CLOSE-HAULED

The closest angle you can sail to the wind is on the edge of the no-go zone. This point of sailing is called close-hauled. You should have the sails pulled in tight with the centreboard pushed fully down to prevent the boat from slipping sideways.

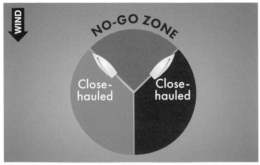

Close-hauled is the closest angle possible to sail into the wind

To maintain this point of sailing, you should continually gently probe with the tiller to find the point where the sails just start to flap and then turn it slightly the other way. Close-hauled is the point of sailing you should use if you want to sail towards the wind.

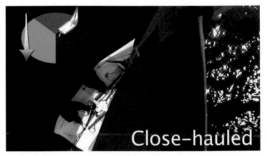

A two-person boat close-hauled: both sails are pulled in tight and the boom is over the corner of the boat

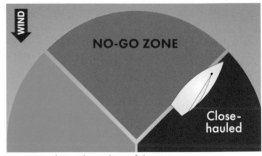

Keep probing the edge of the no-go zone to maintain the close-hauled point of sail

If your destination is straight into the wind, you will be unable to get there directly so you will need to keep switching from one side of the no-go zone to the other. This manoeuvre is called tacking and a series of tacks is called beating. Read the chapter on How to Tack on page XXX for more information on this.

Note: Close-hauled is the only point of sailing where the boat is steered to find the point where the sails flap. The sails are pulled in hard, and the boat is steered gently, until they flutter. On all other points of sailing, the boat is steered to a constant heading and the sails are adjusted to find the point where they stop flapping.

A series of tacks together with close-hauled sailing is called beating

TOP TIP

The wind rarely blows in a consistent direction for more than a few minutes. It is continually shifting. You must look out for these changes of direction by finding the point where the sail just starts to flutter. This ensures that the sail has optimum performance.

Close-hauled sailing often calls for vigorous hiking (leaning out) to balance the boat

REACHING

Reaching is the term used for any point of sailing where the boat is sailing generally across the wind. It covers any angle between 60° and 120° from the direction from which the wind is blowing.

CLOSE REACH

The first reaching point to learn is the close reach. This point of sailing is approximately 60° off the wind. Turn to this direction and release the sails slightly until they just start to flutter. Then pull them back in so they stop flapping at the luff (leading edge) and raise the centreboard or daggerboard about a quarter up.

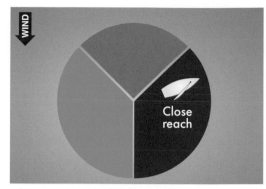

Close reach point of sailing. Ease mainsheet and raise centreboard slightly

Boat close reaching with sails correctly adjusted

BEAM REACH

Next is the beam reach. Here you will be sailing at 90° to the wind. A beam reach is the best point of sailing for your first sail as the sails and the boat are easily controlled and you are well away from the no-go zone. Turn to this position and adjust the sails as before. You should also raise the centreboard so it is about halfway up.

Keep adjusting the mainsheet to find the point where the luff of the sail just stops flapping.

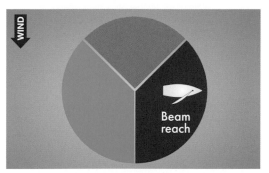

Beam reach point of sailing – boom is 45° to the side of boat and the centreboard is halfway up

BROAD REACH

Another point of sailing is the broad reach. Here you will start to sail slightly away from the wind and be sailing at around 120° off the wind. Release and adjust the sails to find the point where they stop fluttering and raise the centreboard so it's about two-thirds of the way up.

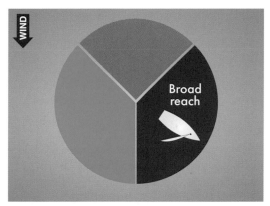

Broad reach point of sailing – boom is eased approximately 60° to the side and centreboard is about two-thirds up

Bird's-eye view of two-person boat on a beam reach

Single-person boat on training run. Boom is 90° to the side of the boat

RUNNING

We now come onto the running points of sailing. Running is when the boat is sailing away from the direction the wind is blowing from. On these points of sailing the wind simply pushes the boat along.

TRAINING RUN

The first running point is called a training run. Here you will be pointing almost directly away from the wind, sailing at an angle of about 150° off the wind.

Release the mainsail so the boom is almost at 90° to the boat, and the centreboard should be about three-quarters of the way up. The only exception to altering the centreboard position is when sailing with an asymmetric spinnaker. Here it is more usual to keep the centreboard fully lowered when sailing on a reach or running point of sailing. For more information on this refer to the Asymmetric Spinnaker chapter on page 147. If sailing a two-person boat, the crew lets out the jib.

When learning, the training run is the best point of sailing if you want to sail away from the wind, as there is less risk of the boom accidentally flipping across, which is called gybing. (For more information, read the How to Gybe chapter on page 123.)

DEAD RUN

The second running and the final point of sailing is a dead run. This is when the boat is pointing directly away from the wind.

While you are learning, this point of sailing is probably best avoided until your wind awareness has developed. It is very easy for the wind to suddenly catch the wrong side of the sail, which can cause the boom to flick across the boat extremely fast in a gybe and capsize you.

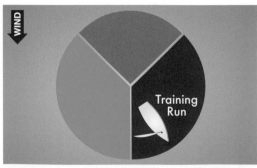

The training run reduces the chance of the boom accidentally flicking across the boat

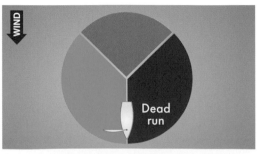

A dead run is sailing directly away from the wind. Be careful of the wind accidentally flicking the boom across

KEY LEARNING POINTS

- **Wind awareness** is a key skill to develop, as the boat's angle to the wind is fundamental to everything that happens on board.

- The **no-go zone** is an area of about 45° either side of where the wind is blowing from and the boat will have no forward drive in this zone. You MUST understand where the no-go zone is relative to your boat at all times and be sure to keep out of the zone.

- **Close-hauled** is on the edge of the no-go zone. Sails are pulled in fully and the centreboard is pushed fully down.

- **Close reach** is approximately 20° away from the close-hauled point of sailing. Sails are set so they just stop flapping. Raise the centreboard a quarter of the way up.

- **Beam reach** is about 90° to the wind. Release the boom so it's approximately 45° over the side of the boat and the sails don't flap. The centreboard should be halfway up.

- **Broad reach** is about 120° to the wind. Sails are set so they are just not flapping. The centreboard is about two-thirds up.

- A **training run** is a further 30° away from a broad reach. The boom is almost 90° to the boat and the centreboard is three-quarters of the way up.

- **Dead run** is sailing directly away from the wind. The boom is 90° to the boat and the centreboard stays at three-quarters up.

- You must understand and establish where the wind is blowing from and adjust your sails and centreboard to suit each point of sailing.

Good wind awareness helps you to identify the correct point of sailing and what that means for the settings

KEY FACTORS

THERE ARE SEVERAL DIFFERENT FACTORS THAT WORK TOGETHER TO ALLOW THE BOAT TO SAIL. WORKING TOGETHER CORRECTLY OPTIMISES PERFORMANCE

Go online for a video demonstration: www.fernhurstbooks.com – search for *Sailing: A Beginner's Guide* and click on 'Additional resources'.

There are several key factors that affect how a sailing dinghy performs. To get the best performance out of your boat and maximise your enjoyment, it is important to understand what these factors are, how to spot them and how, as one changes, it impacts on the others. They are all of equal importance and none can be overlooked or skipped if you want to sail the boat to its best potential.

In time you should aim to develop a good understanding of all the key factors. This will form the foundation of all your learning development and in time they will become second nature. You should keep thinking about them at all times when afloat. Remember that as one factor changes there is a knock-on effect on the others so be prepared to make adjustments all round.

These key factors apply to all sailing craft, whether they are a single-person or a two-person boat and on all points of sailing. Correct understanding of the key factors also helps you to develop good sailing techniques.

The key factors are:
1. SAIL setting
2. Boat BALANCE
3. Boat TRIM
4. COURSE sailed
5. CENTREBOARD position

WIND AWARENESS

Before we look at these five key factors, let's just recap on wind awareness which is above the key factors and is so important to understand and a vital skill to develop but arguably the hardest thing to master. It forms the basis of absolutely everything that happens aboard your boat. It is worth spending time to learn all the ways to spot the wind in terms of direction and strength. This has an impact on how to set the sails, where to sit, and how to react when the wind changes.

Remember that it is easy to become disorientated as you move around the boat, particularly when you alter course. Understanding where the wind is blowing from at all times allows you to help identify what you should be doing.

This was covered in the previous Points of Sailing chapter, but let's recap on how you can be wind aware:

- To help you spot where the wind is blowing from, use a masthead burgee which will point towards the wind.
- Flags ashore are another indicator, they simply flutter along the line that the wind is blowing.
- Ripples or waves on the water also move in a direction from where the wind is coming from.
- A flapping sail is your biggest wind indicator. Release the control sheets and let the sail flap.

The key factors apply on all points of sail

It will act just like a flag and will lie in the same direction that the wind is blowing.

- As a further aid you can also tie strips of wool to the wire shrouds. These will stream out in the direction that the wind is travelling.

NO-GO ZONE

As described in the Points of Sailing chapter (see page 37), the no-go zone is an area that is approximately 45° either side of where the wind is blowing from. You will not be able to sail in this area as the sails don't work and will simply flap. Once you have developed good wind awareness the next step is to learn to identify this zone.

You should try to keep well clear of the no-go zone at all times unless you intend to turn the boat around by tacking across the wind. (See the How to Tack chapter on page 113 on how to do this).

When a boat points head to wind the sails simply flap

WIND STRENGTH

Wind strength is also an important consideration. Think of the wind as the fuel for the boat. If you have too much it will be hard to control the boat. You should only go sailing if you are confident that you can control your boat in the prevailing conditions. It is better to leave things for another day if the wind is too strong for you. Being overpowered can be hazardous and tiring so it is best to limit your development to days when the wind is within your capabilities.

The wind often comes in gusts of stronger wind. When sailing along, you should keep a look out for these gusts of wind coming. These often appear as darker patches of water and can move across the water quickly. Spotting these patches is a good skill to learn as you will be in a good position to anticipate the need to spill wind from the sail by releasing the mainsheet if required when the gust of wind hits. This will reduce the number of capsizes you will endure.

Gusts of wind appear as darker patches on the water

Once you are wind aware, you can consider the five key factors affecting your sailing.

FACTOR 1. SAIL SETTING

Sails are your engine, accelerator and brake all in one, so it is important to have them set properly to ensure you stay in control and maximise your speed.

Correct sail settings are needed on all points of sailing

As we have explained the sail will work on any point of sail that is outside of the no-go zone.

Boats can sail anywhere other than in the no-go zone

CONTROL SHEET

The most obvious sail control is the rope that pulls the sail in and out. These are called sheets. For the mainsail there is a mainsheet and, on a two-person boat, a jibsheet.

Each point of sail requires different settings for these sheets.

The trick is to find the point when the sail just stops flapping. The helmsman should release the mainsheet until the front edge or luff of the mainsail starts to flap. In a two-person boat, the crew adjusts the jibsheet to achieve the same effect.

When this point is reached, pull it in slightly until it stops flapping. The amount you will need to pull the sails in to find this point will vary depending on the point of sailing you are on at the time.

The last part of the sail to fill with wind is the part just behind the mast. On a single-person boat, release the mainsheet until the leading edge of the sail flap. This is called backwinding. When this point is reached pull the sail back in until it stops flapping.

Control sheets pull the sails in and out

The sail flaps just behind the mast on single-person dinghies

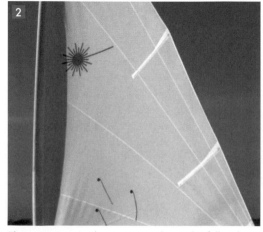

The correct mainsheet tension shows the full sail

On a two-person boat the helmsman does the same and the crew adjusts the jib to find the point where the jib just stops to flap.

Release the mainsheet and jibsheet until the sails flap

Pull the sails in until they stop flapping – this is the optimum position

As the boat turns on to alternative points of sailing the control sheets should be adjusted.

On a beam reach the boom should be released approximately 45° over the side of the boat.

On a beam reach, ease the mainsheet so the boom is 45° out

When on a training run the boom is released further so it is approaching 90° to the boat.

On a training run, ease the mainsheet so the boom is almost 90° out

Telltales

Telltales are small strips normally made of lightweight fabric or wool, and stuck to both sides of the sail, normally about six inches behind the luff of the sail. These can be on the mainsail on a single-person boat and the jib on a two-person boat.

These are here to help you set the sheet tension and the aim is to keep the telltales streaming evenly on both sides of the sail.

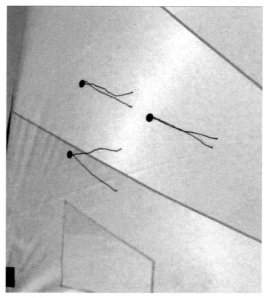

Telltales stream evenly when the sail is correctly set

Telltales react before the flapping point of the sail and respond to subtle amounts of control sheet movement.

If the sail is pulled in too tight for your particular point of sail the outer telltale will flap and stall. If you see this, simply release the sheet until the telltale streams. If you go too far or if the control sheet is too loose the sail will probably be flapping. In this case, pull the sheet in until it stops flapping and then make smaller adjustments to make sure the telltale streams evenly.

Remember: For the best setting for the sail, release the sheet to let the sail out until it flaps, and then pull it in slightly to stop it flapping. Or, looking at the telltales, if the inner telltale is stalled then pull the sail in and if the outer one is stalled then release the sail.

Close-Hauled Sail Setting

Sailing close-hauled is the only point of sailing where things are different. Here the sails are pulled in tight with the boom over the corner of the boat and the boat is steered to find the point where the sails start to flap. This ensures that you remain on the edge of the no-go zone.

Bird's-eye view of a single-person boat sailing close-hauled

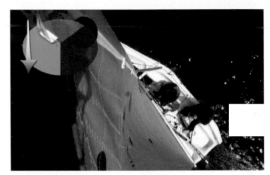

Bird's-eye view of a two-person boat sailing close-hauled

The boom is over the corner of the boat when sailing close-hauled

On a single-person boat steer the boat to find the point where the mainsail just starts to backwind.

On a two-person boat you are looking for the point where the leading edge of the jib just starts to backwind.

When either of these points are reached, simply bear away from the wind slightly by pulling the tiller away from the boom in very small amounts until the sail fills evenly.

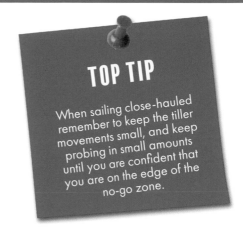

TOP TIP

When sailing close-hauled remember to keep the tiller movements small, and keep probing in small amounts until you are confident that you are on the edge of the no-go zone.

The jib starts to backwind as the boat enters the no-go zone

The jib pops into shape when you bear away out of the no-go zone

And, using the telltales when close-hauled, you pull the sails in tight and steer the boat to make the telltales stream evenly. If you are too close to the no-go zone the inner telltales will stall (i.e. point upwards and flutter significantly), so bear away from the wind just a little. If the outer telltales are stalled (i.e. they hang downwards), then point the bow of the boat (i.e. luff up) towards the no-go zone until the telltales stream evenly.

Overpowered

Close-hauled is the point of sailing that you are most likely to become overpowered. The reason for this is that, with the sails pulled in closer to the centreline of the boat, the wind exerts a large sideways force that will try to tip the boat over at its narrowest point.

The tipping effect is called heeling and when you feel this, release the mainsheet a little.

The wind tries to knock the boat over most when close-hauled

As gusts of wind hit, ease the mainsheet

This frees off the mainsail and dumps some of the power. Consequently, the front edge (luff) of the sail will start to flap and backwind, and the boat should return to a more upright position. This is the only occasion when a flapping sail at the luff edge is acceptable.

Slowing Down

Sails are both your accelerator and, more importantly, your brake. The only way to slow a boat down is to release the sails so they flap. As such they will simply act like a flag and you will slow down and even stop. Learning how to control your speed is arguably the most important skill in sailing. It is no good tearing around if you are unable to reduce your speed, and quickly, if need be, for example when approaching another vessel or hazard.

OTHER SAIL CONTROLS

There are a few other sail controls that relate to the key factor of sail setting and are important to understand how to use. These are:

Clew Outhaul

The clew outhaul is the control line that pulls the bottom edge or foot of the sail along the boom. This is connected to the clew (bottom, aft corner) of the sail.

The clew outhaul needs to be reasonably tight. As a rough guide, pull it out so that at the mid-point of the boom you have approximately 5cm of curve in the sail. This will provide the maximum drive.

If the wind is stronger, you can pull the outhaul tighter to reduce the curve in the lower part of the sail. This depowers the sail slightly and helps you to keep control in the gusts.

Kicking Strap (Or Vang)

The kicking strap or vang is the control that, when tight, prevents the boom from rising when the mainsheet is released. It controls the tension on the trailing edge or leech of the sail and is mainly used when sailing on the close-hauled point of sailing, particularly when windy. It should, however, be eased slightly when bearing away from the wind onto a reaching or running point of sail.

As already seen on page 17, the kicking strap can be configured to either pull or push the boom down. Whatever system your boat has, the effect is the same: the boom is prevented from rising when the mainsheet is released.

If the kicking strap is too slack when the mainsheet is released, the boom rises, allowing more curve along the leech, which in turn makes the boat harder to control.

Correct outhaul tension on the left; too loose on the right

The kicking strap controls the leech tension – the correct tension is on the left; too loose on the right

When the kicking strap is tight, as the mainsheet is released the leech of the sail is held more rigidly and the whole sail moves out as if it were a flat board. This makes the boat easier to control.

The best way to set the kicking strap for the close-hauled point of sailing is to first pull the mainsheet in hard so the boom is positioned over the corner of the boat and then take all the slack out of the kicking strap control line.

When you turn away from the close-hauled point of sailing, try to remember to release the kicking strap by a few centimetres. This opens up the leech of the sail, which will generate a little more power in the sail.

When sailing upwind, pull the kicking strap tight

When sailing away from the wind, ease the kicking strap slightly

Cunningham Or Downhaul

The final control line to understand is the cunningham or downhaul. This is a control line that loops through a reinforced eyelet just above the boom near the mast.

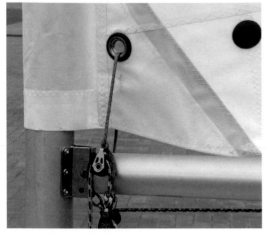

Cunningham eyelet by the mast

It pulls the leading edge of the sail down a little and has a subtle effect on the top part of the leech of the mainsail. The cunningham / downhaul should only be used in stronger winds as it depowers the sail slightly.

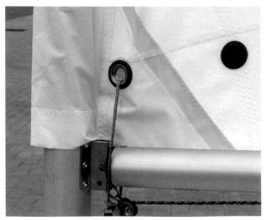

When tensioned, this subtle control makes the boat easier to sail in windy conditions

To start with, this control is hard to identify so don't worry too much about it; all you need to know is that the stronger the wind is, the more you pull it.

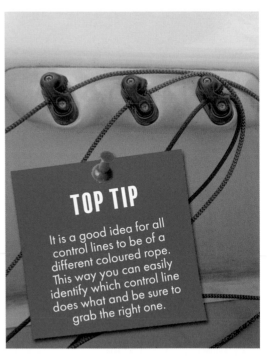

TOP TIP

It is a good idea for all control lines to be of a different coloured rope. This way you can easily identify which control line does what and be sure to grab the right one.

TOP TIP

Try to remember the settings you use each time for the clew outhaul, kicking strap and cunningham, and judge the performance of the boat. Different wind strengths need different settings. To help you remember what works for you, stick numbered adhesive strips as a measuring tool for each control.

FACTOR 2: BOAT BALANCE

The next key factor is balance of the boat.

You should aim to sail the boat as flat as you can. This is easy to say but hard to achieve. The reason for this is that fundamentally sailboats sail best when they are level in the water with little or no heel. It is often more comfortable to sit on a heeling boat, but it is a bad habit.

Try to imagine there is a spirit level running sideways across the boat:

- When the boat is flat, the waterline shape is symmetrical, and the centreboard sits in the middle of this underwater profile
- When the boat heels over, it distorts the underwater shape, forcing the boat to turn towards the wind

To keep sailing in a straight line when heeled, you will need to apply the rudder to counter this turning force. This creates drag and will slow you down. In some cases, the rudder will stall and steering will be lost.

So when you feel the boat being overpowered by a gust of wind, you should ease the mainsheet so the leading edge of the mainsail backwinds. This reduces the effectiveness of the sail and the boat should become level once more.

To help balance the boat you can also lean out, using the toestraps to take your weight. These are strong fabric straps permanently rigged to the boat, under which you hook your feet. If you are sailing a two-person boat, try to work as a team and be sure to use the toestraps.

View from above	**View from underwater**

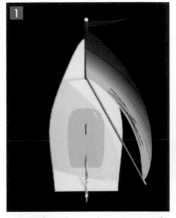 

When flat, the underwater profile of the boat is symmetrical

 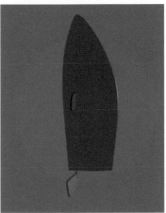

When heeled, the underwater shape is distorted

 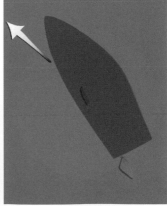

An uneven hull shape forces the boat to turn towards the wind, which is corrected by the rudder, therefore causing drag

Use toestraps to help lean out

Be aware that the wind has a habit of wavering in direction and altering in strength as gusts of wind come and go. You must constantly move your weight in and out to balance the boat, which is great exercise.

Some performance boats have a trapeze for the crew. Here the crew wears a harness with a hook that clips onto an extra wire running parallel to the shroud of the boat. With his weight supported by this wire and harness, the crew then steps onto the side of the boat and pushes out to lie flat. This gets his centre of gravity further out from the boat, which combats the tipping effect of the stronger wind.

TOP TIP

Try to keep the boat flat at all times. This will reduce the amount of rudder that needs to be applied to keep sailing straight. Remember, a rudder is a good brake!

The crew on the trapeze

FACTOR 3: BOAT TRIM

The next factor is boat trim. In simple terms trim is the amount of fore and aft tilt on the boat. If you sit too far back, the rear of the boat, which is called the transom, goes below the water. This upsets the underwater shape of the boat and increases the amount of drag, which therefore slows you down.

Sitting too far back causes drag

When learning how to sail, people often sit too far back and hold the tiller rather than the tiller extension. This may feel more comfortable but is another bad habit. You should practise using the tiller extension at all times, which also encourages you to sit forward.

The only exception to this is when you are more advanced and sailing in strong winds. The boat is then subject to different forces and can easily adopt a condition called planing, which is sailing at its fastest.

Only sit at the back of the boat when planing is possible

In this situation, the power of the wind lifts the nose of the boat clear of the water, leaving just the rear section of the boat in contact with the water, and the speed rises dramatically. This usually happens on the reaching points of sailing when a gust hits. When you feel the gust hit, slide your weight back a little to promote planing.

Sit well forward and hold the tiller extension

FACTOR 4: COURSE SAILED

The next factor is course sailed. Your aim is to sail on the best or shortest course possible for your intended destination.

It is very easy to get distracted and disorientated when sailing and not pay correct attention to where you are actually trying to sail to.

Keep looking out of the boat to check you are still sailing in the right direction and pick a point on the shore as your reference, adjusting your steering to maintain a course to that point.

If you are sailing close-hauled, pull the sails in tight and steer the boat to find the edge of the no-go zone. This will ensure you sail the shortest distance upwind in a series of small steps rather than going backwards and forwards on a series of tight reaches that feel fast but won't be making much headway towards your upwind destination.

Pick a target destination and always sail towards it

Keep your head out of the boat to see where you are going

WINDSHIFTS

The wind rarely blows in a consistent direction for longer than a couple of minutes. This is particularly noticeable on a close-hauled point of sailing when the no-go zone shifts as the wind changes.

When sailing close-hauled, it is a combination of reading these small windshifts and looking out for your landmark that allows you to sail upwind in the most efficient manner.

FACTOR 5: CENTREBOARD POSITION

The final factor is centreboard position. The centreboard is the large plate located in the middle of the boat, which can either slide up or down or pivot around a pin. It is stored inside the hull of the boat (see page 14).

The purpose of the centreboard is to stop the boat slipping sideways, particularly on the close-hauled point of sailing. When close-hauled, most of the energy from the wind will try to blow the boat sideways. To reduce this, push the centreboard fully down.

The centreboard reduces sideways slip when sailing close-hauled

As you progressively bear away from the wind, the direction of this force moves more towards the direction of travel of the boat. This means less sideways force is in play.

On a beam reach the centreboard should be halfway up and on a training run approximately three quarters up.

The reason for this is that the centreboard has a large surface area in contact with the water when fully down, which introduces a fair amount of drag that slows the boat down. As the driving force of the wind moves forward while the boat bears away from the wind, the requirement to prevent sideways slip is reduced. You can therefore lessen the drag by raising the centreboard.

A common trap is to leave the centreboard in one fixed position for all points of sailing.

Remember that when the sails are pulled in, push the centreboard down, and when the sails are out, take the centreboard up by the correct amount.

As a boat bears away from wind, the sideways force moves forward, meaning less centreboard is needed (less drag)

KEY LEARNING POINTS

All the key factors are equally important. You must develop an understanding and pay attention to all of them at all times. Bear in mind that nothing stays the same for long. As one factor changes there is a knock-on effect with all of the others. This is particularly true when you change from one point of sailing to another.

Wind awareness: Wind awareness is a skill to learn and vital to understand as it is fundamental to everything that happens on a boat. Use burgees, flags, flapping sails or ripples on the water to tell you where the wind is coming from.

The wind has a zone in which you can't sail. This is called the no-go zone and is about 45° either side of where the wind is blowing from.

The 5 key factors are
1. **Sail setting**: If the sails are too tight or too slack, the boat will slow down.
   - For optimum speed, release the sail until it just starts to flap and then tighten it again until it just stops flapping
   - Pull the clew outhaul so there is a maximum 5cm curve in the sail at the mid-point of the boom
   - Use the kicking strap when sailing upwind, particularly when windy
   - Pull on the cunningham or downhaul progressively as the wind starts to overpower the boat

2. **Boat balance**: For optimum speed your boat should be flat in the water. Use your weight to balance the boat and be prepared to release the mainsheet to keep the boat flat. You may need to move your weight quickly if the wind gusts or drops suddenly.

3. **Boat trim**: This is the amount of fore or aft tilt the boat has in the water. Make sure you use the tiller extension to control the rudder. This will ensure that you sit well forward.

4. **Course sailed**: Sail the shortest distance to your intended destination. Keep looking out of the boat to check you are still sailing where you need to get to.

5. **Centreboard position**: This foil stops the boat slipping sideways when sailing close-hauled but does also introduce drag. When close-hauled, the centreboard should be fully down. On a beam reach it should be about halfway up; on a training run about three quarters up.

YOUR SAILING ENVIRONMENT & SAFETY

SAFETY AFLOAT IS YOUR PRIORITY & THIS EXTENDS TO WHERE YOU SAIL. WEAR THE RIGHT CLOTHING TO SUIT THE WEATHER FOR YOUR PARTICULAR ENVIRONMENT

Sailing is a fun sport enjoyed by millions in a variety of environments – inland, on the sea, on lakes and rivers, in fact anywhere there is a large patch of water. The environment in which you sail is a vital consideration before going afloat.

Sailing is best enjoyed in a safe environment

Sailing in unsuitable conditions can be dangerous and should be avoided. You must only sail in an area where you can control the boat comfortably. This chapter looks at the sailing environment and what you should wear when sailing.

The golden rule of sailing is NEVER sail alone. A quiet and deserted stretch of water may look inviting and a good place to learn alone, but hidden hazards or currents could exist. You must choose a location where other boats are sailing.

The best places are recognised clubs that can provide assistance if required, should you get into difficulties. You will also receive expert local knowledge of the area from practically every club member, so this is another reason to sail at a recognised sailing club.

You should keep clear of any large commercial shipping as they cannot alter course easily.

Unexposed rocks and sandbanks may also be a problem.

Only sail where other boats are present

Be wary of other water users

BUOYANCY AIDS

A personal flotation device must be worn at all times when on or near the water. Even if you are a very confident swimmer you can be dunked quickly into cold, deep water and clothing will hinder your ability to swim.

Most dinghy sailors wear a buoyancy aid that will help to keep them afloat when they are in the water. These are comfortable to wear and allow free body movement as you move around the boat. It is important to understand that these vests will not keep you face up in the unlikely event of being knocked unconscious. If you are worried about this then a full lifejacket should be worn.

Lifejackets tend to be bulky and cumbersome to wear on a dinghy and they will restrict your movement around the boat.

The vast majority of people opt for the buoyancy aid. You must wear your buoyancy aid tightly so it doesn't come off when you fall in the water.

Lifejackets can be cumbersome but offer more buoyancy

Buoyancy aids are snug fitting

WINDS

You should pay attention to weather forecasts, and in particular to what the wind strength and direction is likely to be in your area for the time you plan to sail. Forecasts are available from local press, radio and television as well as internet or mobile phone applications.

You must always understand your level of ability and respect the elements. Do not sail if the wind is strong until you have learnt the basics on fair weather days.

Strong winds can create big waves

WIND SPEED

To help judge the wind speed there is a recognised wind measurement scale called the Beaufort scale. This comprises bands of wind force strengths, starting at zero and going up to hurricane force 12.

To begin with you should limit your sailing to fair weather days where there is a moderate breeze of no more than force 4 or 16 knots (28kph).

BEAUFORT SCALE

	Calm	Light air	Light breeze	Gentle breeze	Moderate	Fresh breeze	Strong breeze	Moderate gale	Fresh gale
	0	1	2	3	4	5	6	7	>8
Knots	0	1-3	4-6	7-10	11-16	17-21	22-27	28-33	>34

The Beaufort scale measures wind speed

As your experience grows you will be able to cope with the demands of stronger winds. It is better to have an enjoyable sailing session and learn a bit more each time than risk sailing in unsuitable conditions.

Fair weather days are ideal as there is a reasonable breeze on these days and you will get a good feel for how the boat is driven by the wind. On fair weather days, flags flutter gently in the breeze and the water should look relatively smooth. A wind of around force three to four (wind up to 16 knots) provides ideal conditions in which to learn how to sail.

Flags on a medium wind strength day

Avoid strong winds until your experience has grown. If faced with this situation, you must not go afloat.

A flag on a strong wind day

Do not sail in a thunderstorm, as the mast is an excellent lightning conductor. If you get caught out in one, you must return to shore. As mentioned earlier, before you go afloat you should obtain a good weather forecast for your area.

LEE SHORE

This is the term used to describe the beach or area of land onto which the wind is blowing. It can be hard to sail away from a lee shore as the wind will always try to blow you back on to it. We explain more on how to launch from a lee shore in the Beach Launching & Recovery chapter on page 75, but when out sailing you must identify which area is likely to be the lee shore and keep well away from it.

TIDES

If you are sailing on the sea you must be aware of the tide and what that means to you. The tide comes in and out twice a day, taking approximately 12 hours for one complete cycle. Information on tide times comes in a variety of sources. Weather and tide information is generally available online, in local media, on a smart phone app or on the wall of your local sailing club.

Weather and tide forecasts are available in a variety of places

The cycle of the moon has an effect on the tide times and the tidal range, which is the difference in height between high water and low water.

When there is either a full or new moon, the earth, the sun and the moon are all in a line and Spring tides come into effect. On a Spring tide the tidal range is increased with higher high-water levels and lower low-water levels.

When the moon is in half phase it sits to one side of the line between the earth and the sun, and Neap tides come into effect, resulting in a smaller tidal range.

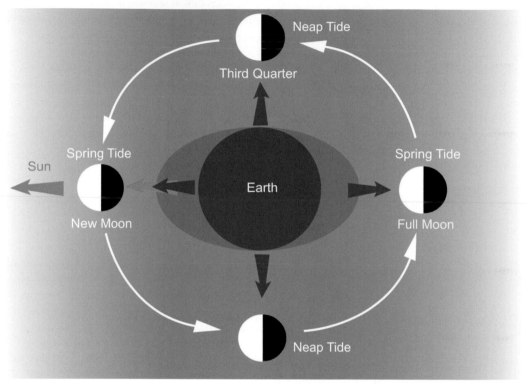

The phase of the moon has different effects on the tidal range. New and full moon has Spring tides which are stronger than Neap tides which are at half phase

As well as the impact of the moon, tidal ranges also vary depending on your location and the atmospheric pressure. So research your particular area and understand what the tides and weather are doing during the period in which you plan to sail.

As the tide comes in and out, the current in the water changes direction (by as much as 180°) and speed. The current can exceed the speed your boat is capable of reaching when sailing; bear in mind that if you haven't researched the tides properly you could be swept out to sea if the wind drops.

Water currents can exceed the speed of a boat

Tidal currents get particularly strong at harbour entrances and headlands, therefore avoid sailing in these areas.

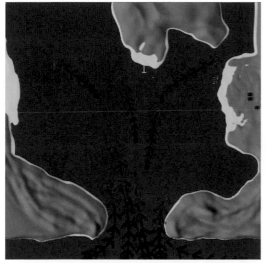

Tidal flows are strongest at harbour entrances

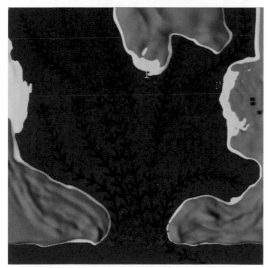

Tidal flow changes direction depending on the state of the rise, potentially pushing you out to sea

Currents also exist in rivers, so if you plan to sail on a river you must find out what the directional flow of the current is going to be. The speed of the current is also affected by the amount of recent rainwater as this can swell the volume of water in the river.

BOAT CONDITION

Your boat must be in a seaworthy condition and be fully watertight. If you are in doubt, you must get the boat checked by a professional. You should regularly check the hull for cracks and holes and get these repaired as a matter of urgency. You should also regularly inspect any wire rigging that the boat has and replace parts of this if there are obvious signs of wear.

Make sure your boat is in good condition and repair any damage immediately

Wooden boats may need a coat of new paint or varnish to keep the wood in good condition.

Buoyancy tanks have plastic inspection hatches that should be well fitted, while drainage holes are inserted at the back of the boat to allow you to drain any water that may collect in the buoyancy tanks while sailing. For more information on buoyancy tanks and drainage holes see page 12.

Boats have in-built buoyancy in the construction

EQUIPMENT

It's a good idea to carry a paddle on board that you can use if the wind drops, a long piece of rope in case you need to be towed, a whistle to attract attention, a sharp safety knife, a sponge and a bailer to allow you to scoop out any water that may collect in the boat. A small anchor is sensible if you are sailing on the sea and you may also consider carrying a small flare pack. Your local chandler should be able to provide specific advice on these.

Other equipment to have aboard; also consider carrying a safety knife

Carry a paddle in case the wind dies

CLOTHING

What you wear is also very important. You must wear clothing to suit the climate in your particular area, whether it be hot or cold. This will range from shorts and t-shirts in warmer climates to wetsuits and even drysuits in the winter months.

Chandlers stock a wide range of suitable clothing. Most nautical clothing is made from man-made fibres and is ideally suited for sailing. These types of fabrics are light to wear, flexible when worn and yet still offer warmth when wet. They also dry quickly.

It is best to wear a series of thin layers that could be adjusted if needed. Being too hot is just as much of a hazard as being too cold.

To help keep the wind and spray off you, you should wear a waterproof layer. It will also help to keep you warm. This layer can either be a one-

TOP TIP

- Use a plastic four litre milk container cut in half as a bailer. This is much cheaper than one from a shop, works just as well and is easy to replace when lost.

- Make sure that any loose items are tied on to the boat so that you don't lose them if you capsize.

piece suit or top and trousers. Breathable fabrics are best for these items as they are far more comfortable to wear than non-breathable items.

Bear in mind that even on a sunny day, if it is windy the spray will cool you down significantly, which could be uncomfortable, so a spray top is well advised.

Do not wear natural fibres such as wool or cotton – they are heavy when wet and don't dry quickly

If you decide to sail in cold areas or over the winter, you may consider a drysuit. These suits are designed to keep the water out and have flexible seals around the neck and wrists. It is also usual for them to have integrated socks. They work by keeping you dry and, when worn in conjunction with a series of thin layers underneath, you can dress according to the temperature you are in.

In cold weather more than 50 percent of heat loss is through the head, so wear a warm hat.

Wear a hat if it's cold

Windproof tops keep the wind and spray off

A wetsuit is a sensible option if you plan to sail on windy days or when the weather is inclement. Wetsuits are made from stretchy neoprene and should be tight fitting. When wet, they work by trapping a layer of water in the suit next to the skin, which heats up quickly. Wetsuits are flexible to wear and also offer great protection from knocks and bangs as well as from the sun.

TOP TIP

It is important to wear your buoyancy aid as the outermost garment of clothing. This will allow somebody to grab hold of it easily to help pull you back aboard in the event of a capsize or safety boat rescue.

Wetsuits trap a layer of water in the suit that acts as insulation

Buoyancy aid must be the outermost garment in case you need two be dragged back on board

PROTECTING FEET, HANDS & HEAD

Footwear is important. Try to avoid sailing barefoot. You can easily stub your toe moving around the boat or cut it on an exposed sharp area. Non-slip footwear is a practical choice and a wide selection is available from chandlers.

Ropes can burn your hands if you let them slide through your fingers, so wearing sailing gloves is a sensible idea.

Some people opt to wear safety helmets to protect them from bangs, usually from the boom.

Good footwear is important. Non-slip shoes or boots are best

Safety helmets are advisable for children

Ropes can burn your hands if they slip through, so wear gloves

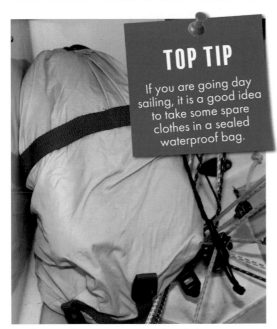

Wear plastic sunglasses when sunny to reduce the glare

Dehydration is a factor that also needs to be considered. Sailing is a physically active sport, and you can lose a lot of moisture through perspiration after even moderate effort. Take out something to drink in a plastic bottle and carry a few snacks aboard too.

Make sure that you store any dry clothes in a waterproof bag

BEWARE OF THE SUN

You must be careful of the sun's rays. The wind and spray can mask the burning power of the UV light, particularly on a windy day. Even with cloud cover, the UV light can still get through and is also intensified by reflections off the water.

Take suncream afloat with you and apply it regularly to exposed areas of skin. A hat with a peak is also useful.

If you wear sunglasses, ensure that these are made of plastic and fit a restraining strap to the arms of the glasses in case they fall off.

NEXT STEPS

Safety afloat should be your paramount concern. Do not feel embarrassed if you decide not to go out if the environment or weather does not suit you.

Make sure you understand the weather forecast and research the tide times if you are sailing on the sea. Also, research other local environmental aspects that may affect your area.

Familiarise yourself with websites that will give you information about the weather and tides for the area in which you are likely to sail. This way you will get used to reading and interpreting information for different weather conditions and tide times.

Practise being able to read the wind strength by fluttering flags and ripples on the water.

KEY LEARNING POINTS

- Understand your level of ability
- Respect the elements
- Always wear a personal buoyancy aid
- Never sail alone
- Understand the tide times and weather forecast
- Make sure your boat is seaworthy
- Wear clothing to suit your particular environment in layers that can be adjusted as your temperature varies
- The wind can mask the power of the sun's rays so you should use sun cream to protect exposed skin

BEACH LAUNCHING & RECOVERY

CORRECT LAUNCHING & RECOVERY WILL AVOID DAMAGE TO THE BOAT OR INJURY TO YOURSELF

Go online for a video demonstration: www.fernhurstbooks.com – search for *Sailing: A Beginner's Guide* and click on 'Additional resources'.

Dinghies can be sailed in a variety of locations – on lakes, rivers and coastal waters. Launching and recovery is an important element to master as it is easy to damage a boat or cause injury if done incorrectly.

This chapter looks at how to launch and return to a beach. The main difference between beach launching and pontoon launching (see page 89) is that it is normal to hoist the sails on the beach before the boat is put into the water.

The basic principles apply to both single-person and two-person dinghies. With a single-person dinghy, you will need to find assistance from a friend or fellow sailor to park and retrieve your trolley.

BEACH LAUNCHING

Before launching, first you need to establish the direction the wind is blowing from. To help you judge where the wind is coming from you can use a masthead burgee, which will point towards the wind. Other useful indicators can be flags ashore or ripples on the water, which move in the same direction as the wind.

Identify where the wind is blowing from

When learning, try to avoid launching if there are big waves, as they can easily knock the boat over when you leave the beach. If you are sailing in coastal regions, you must establish what time high water is as the tide may come in during your sail (see page 67).

A seaweed mark on the beach is a good indication of where the water can rise to. It is important to put anything you intend to leave on the beach above the high-water mark to ensure it is still there on your return.

Park the trolley above the high-water line on the beach

There are three main wind directions on a beach that you need to consider. These are:
- **Onshore** winds, which blow onto the beach
- **Cross-shore** winds, which blow parallel to the beach
- **Offshore** winds, which blow away from the beach

Regardless of the wind direction, in all beach launches you should position your boat on its trolley, with the bow of the boat pointing towards the wind.

For more details on how to hoist the sails, refer to the Rigging chapter on page 23.

Fit the rudder, securing the safety pin, and ensure all the drainage bungs are in place to stop the buoyancy tanks from filling with water when afloat.

Position the boat on the beach so the bow is pointing into the wind

Rig and hoist the sails. Make sure the mainsheet and kicking strap are completely slack to allow the boom to flutter in the wind, which keeps the sail loose and unpowered, preventing the boat from blowing off the trolley accidentally.

Fit the rudder

Ensure the safety clip for the rudder is fitted and check all drainage bungs are in

ONSHORE WIND

This is where the wind is blowing onto the beach. Sometimes called a lee shore, it is the hardest beach to launch from as the wind will always try to blow you back ashore.

In this situation, when you face the water you should feel the wind blowing onto your face.

With the sails hoisted, introduce the boat to the water, keeping the bow head to wind. This will keep the sails flapping and make manoeuvring easy.

Continue walking the boat into the water until it floats off the trolley.

A slack mainsheet and kicking strap allow the mainsail to flutter in the wind

Single-Person Beach Launching

If sailing a single-person dinghy, it is possible for one person to hold two boats whilst the other parks both trolleys ashore.

- Ensure the trolley is left above the high-water mark, which is usually indicated by a line of seaweed on the beach
- Lean into the boat and push the centreboard down, but just a little to avoid it hitting the bottom when in shallow water
- Next push the rudder blade down a few inches to allow the tip of the blade to make contact with the water

- Grab the tiller extension and mainsheet; you are now ready to go
- Take one last look around to check the area is clear
- With the bow of the boat pointing head to wind, you will be in the centre of the no-go zone and unable to sail
- To get going, push the boat clear of the no-go zone onto a close reach point of sailing, with the sails still flapping

Make sure you push the boat so you end up on the side opposite the boom. This makes it easier to

Walk the boat bow first into the water

Walk until the boat floats off the trolley

Insert the centreboard slightly to stop it hitting the bottom

Lower the tip of the rudder blade into the water

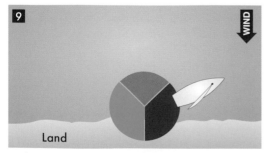

A close reach keeps you well clear of the no-go zone

Climb aboard holding the tiller extension

climb aboard. If you push the boat the other way and end up under the boom, there is a good chance you will capsize the boat as you climb in!

Climb aboard and gently pull the mainsail in a little bit to get moving, but as the rudder isn't fully down you should leave the beach slowly and steering should feel very heavy.

Once you are in an adequate depth of water, you can lower the rudder blade. This is best done with the boat stationary. Release the mainsheet so that the sail flaps to stop the boat and lower the rudder blade fully. Then secure the downhaul rope to keep it in position.

Finally, lower the centreboard to suit your point of sailing, pull the sail back in and sail away.

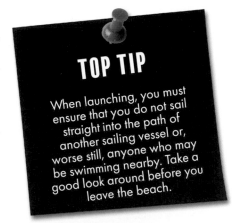

TOP TIP

When launching, you must ensure that you do not sail straight into the path of another sailing vessel or, worse still, anyone who may be swimming nearby. Take a good look around before you leave the beach.

One person can hold two boats while the other takes the trolleys ashore

If sailing on tidal waters, park the trolley above the seaweed mark

Grab the tiller extension and check the area is clear

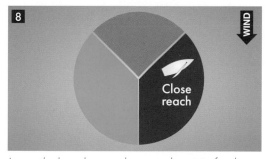

Leave the beach on a close reach point of sailing

Sail away slowly

When in deep enough water, lower the rudder fully

Two-Person Beach Launch

There are many similarities between launching a one-person and two-person boat, but having another pair of hands makes things slightly easier.

- Park the boat on the beach, with the bow head to wind
- Hoist the sails and ensure the mainsheet and kicking strap are loose
- Fit the rudder and check the drainage bungs are in place

For more information on rigging the sails, refer to the Rigging chapter on page 23.

- Walk the boat into the water, keeping the bow head to wind
- Float the boat off the trolley and ask the crew to park this above the high-water mark
- When the crew returns, he holds the boat whilst you climb aboard

- When aboard, lower the centreboard and rudder blade slightly to allow you to sail to deeper water but without touching the bottom
- Next, unfurl the jib if you haven't done so already, keeping the bow head to wind

As with the single-person boat, the best angle to sail away from the beach is on the close reach point of sailing, so ask the crew to turn the bow onto this point. Pick up the tiller extension and instruct the crew to climb aboard from the side opposite the boom.

Sail away slowly, bearing in mind that the steering will be heavy as the rudder is still raised.

When adequate depth is reached, slow the boat by letting the sails flap and then lower the rudder. Finally lower the centreboard to suit the point of sailing you plan to use (see Points of Sailing chapter on page 37) and sail away.

Keeping the boat head to wind, walk the boat into the water

The crew takes the trolley above the high-water mark while the helmsman holds the boat

The helmsman gets in and lowers the centreboard and the tip of the rudder blade slightly

The crew keeps the boat head to wind until you are ready to leave

Once the crew climbs aboard, sail away slowly on a close reach

Lower the rudder blade and centreboard when in deep water

TOP TIP

Ensure you take a landmark on the part of the beach that you leave from. From just a few hundred metres out, it is easy to forget where you started from and where the trolley is!

CROSS-SHORE WIND

A cross-shore wind is where the wind is blowing parallel to the beach. This is probably the easiest beach to launch from and recover to as you simply sail straight out and in.

On this beach, all the preparations are still done with the bow pointing head to wind, but this time the boat is parked parallel to the water.

- With the bow pointing into the wind, hoist the sails, fit the rudder and check the bungs are fitted as before.
- Walk the boat into the water and float it off

the trolley, keeping the bow head to wind.
- As the wind is cross-shore you should walk into the water at a shallow angle. This keeps the sails in the no-go zone.
- Next, allow the boat to float clear of the trolley and return this to shore.
- Take one final check that the area is clear and then either grab the tiller extension and mainsheet, if sailing a single-person dinghy, or climb aboard if sailing a two-person boat.
- Keep the mainsheet slack. Turn the bow of the boat out of the no-go zone onto a beam reach point of sailing. The bow will now be pointing away from the beach.
- As you turn the boat, climb aboard on the side opposite the boom. Pull in a small amount of sail to allow you to slowly sail away from the beach.
- As before, when the water is deep enough, release the sails so they flap and the boat slows down.
- Then fully lower the rudder blade, securing it in place, and lower the centreboard to suit the point of sail you intend to use and sail away.

Walk the boat into the water with the bow head to wind

Hold the boat head to wind

Turn the boat onto a beam reach before you climb in

Grab the tiller extension and mainsheet before you climb aboard

Lower the rudder blade when the water is deep enough

OFFSHORE WIND

Here the wind is blowing away from the beach.

With this wind direction you must be very wary of an additional hazard. It can be deceptively sheltered on this type of beach, as the wind is blowing away from you, and the launch area is often protected by land or buildings. The water may look very flat and safe, but a short way off the shore it can be very rough.

Offshore winds are not the ideal beach to launch from as the wind will blow you away from the shore if you get into difficulty. You should only launch here if you are confident in your abilities to sail back to the beach by beating; if not you will not be able to return to shore.

As with the other wind directions, hoist the sails with the boat facing into the wind on the beach and then introduce the boat into the water and float it clear. Park the trolley ashore and lower the tip of the rudder and centreboard. Make sure the mainsheet and kicking strap are completely slack.

Next, turn the boat onto a beam reach, ensuring you end up on the side opposite the boom. Here the boat will be pointing parallel to the beach. Do one final check that the area is clear.

Grab the tiller extension and mainsheet and climb in, pull in the mainsheet a little and sail away. Turn the boat onto a training run to get you into deeper water. When you've reached the deeper water, turn the boat back into the no-go zone to stop it and lower the rudder blade and centreboard to suit the point of sail you intend to use; then sail away.

BEACH RECOVERY

As with launching, the wind can be either onshore, cross-shore or offshore. Whatever the wind direction, it is vital to approach the beach slowly, controlling your speed by releasing the mainsheet so the sail flaps. Keep a lookout for swimmers and other water users.

When you are about 20 metres or so from the beach, you should slow the boat by letting the sails flap and half raise the rudder blade and centreboard to allow you to sail into shallower water.

Note that once the rudder blade has been

Approach the beach slowly, looking out for swimmers

Half raise the centreboard

On the final approach, prepare to stop the boat

raised, steering will become heavy, and the boat will not manoeuvre as easily.

On any approach to the beach, once you reach shallow water stop the boat by deliberately turning into the no-go zone and then step into the shallow water.

It is your choice as to whether you lower the mainsail with the boat in the water or wait until it is lifted out. Whichever way you choose, keep the bow of the boat head to wind in the middle of the no-go zone before lowering the sail.

With the mainsail lowered, disconnect the halyard and secure this to the shroud and roll the sail up from the head.

Half raise the rudder blade

Continue to approach the beach slowly

Turn into the no-go zone to stop the boat

If you are leaving the boat unattended for any time, it is a good idea to wrap the mainsheet around the boom to stop the wind catching the lowered sail and blowing it onto the dirty sand.

Float the boat onto the trolley and secure the painter. Walk the boat ashore, maintaining the boat head to wind if you have not already lowered the sail. When clear of the water, park the trolley above the high-water mark before you leave the boat unattended in case the tide rises while you are away.

If in a single-person boat, release the clew of the mainsail to allow the sail to flap, and then lift the whole mast out of the boat and lay it flat on the deck of the boat.

ONSHORE WIND

This is where the wind is blowing onto the beach. You must avoid coming ashore on a dead run as you will not be able to control your speed and the wind will simply drive you up the beach. There is also a risk that you may damage the boat.

The best point of sail to approach is the broad reach. This will allow you to control your speed and also turn into the no-go zone and stop when you need to.

As mentioned, raise the rudder and centreboard before your final approach and control your speed.

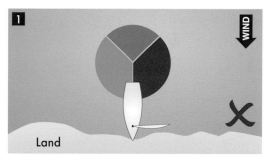

Do not approach the beach on a dead run

A broad reach is the best approach angle as you can slow the boat easily

Finally position the boat in the centre of the no-go zone to stop

Keep looking over the side of the boat into the water and try to judge when the water is shallow enough for you to stand up in it. Other sailors may also be in the area, so this is a good guide. When reached, release the mainsheet and kicking strap and turn the boat back into the no-go zone to stop. You then climb into the water.

The crew should furl the jib, if sailing a two-person boat, and then recover the boat onto the trolley and manoeuvre it clear of the water. In the case of a single-person dinghy, ask somebody nearby to retrieve your trolley.

An alternative recovery procedure for a two-person dinghy when the wind is blowing on shore is to lower the mainsail afloat and sail in under the jib alone.

To do this when the boat is about 50 metres from the shore adopt the hove-to position. Put the boat on a close reach point of sailing, ask the crew to release the jib and pull it across on the wrong side. Release the mainsheet so the mainsail flaps and half raise the centerboard. The boat should stop. With the helmsman keeping the boat steady the crew then lowers the mainsail, rolls the sail up and stores it out of the way in the boat.

Turn the boat towards the shore and sail in under the jib alone. This will force your approach to be slow. When you reach shallow water, the crew hops over the side to steady the boat. The boat is then recovered onto the trolley and taken out of the water.

With the boat hove-to, lower the mainsail

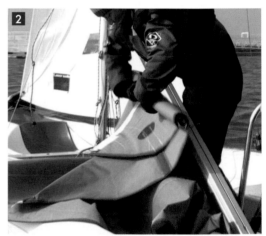

Roll the lowered sail up

The boat is steered to the beach under jib alone

In shallow water the crew furls the jib and steps ashore

The equivalent technique for a single-person dinghy is to:

- Sail parallel to the shore, about 30 metres out.
- Turn into the wind (A in the diagram) and undo the knot in either end of the mainsheet. This will let the boom blow freely, with the sail flapping.
- Point the boat towards the shore and let it drift in. The sail will blow forwards; the wind pressure on the mast is all that is pushing the boat ashore. If you are still going too fast trail a leg in the water as a brake.
- At the last minute, take out the centreboard and step into the water. Then proceed as above.

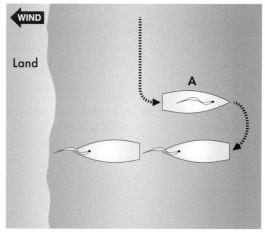

Landing with an onshore wind

Sail towards the shore on a run

Turn head to wind and undo the knot at the end of the mainsheet

Slowly sail in with the sail blowing forwards

Raise the centreboard as you slowly sail towards the shore

CROSS-SHORE WIND

This is where the wind is blowing parallel to the beach. It is probably the easiest beach to land on as you simply sail straight in on a beam reach point of sail.

Approach the beach slowly, with the rudder and centreboard half raised. When you reach shallow water, release the mainsheet and kicking strap and turn the boat into the no-go zone, as already explained. Step into the shallow water, recover the trolley and take the boat out as previously shown.

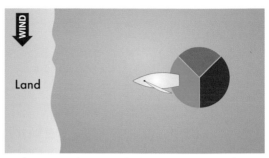

With a cross-shore wind a boat can sail straight towards the beach

OFFSHORE WIND

This is where the wind is blowing away from the shore. You will not be able to point the boat straight at the beach here as you will enter the no-go zone and be blown away from the shore if you do. You should approach the beach on a close-hauled point of sailing, being careful to keep clear of the no-go zone.

As with the other wind directions, when you are about 20 metres out, stop the boat by letting the sails flap and part raise the centreboard and rudder. Approach the beach slowly, keeping an eye out for swimmers.

You will still be sailing close-hauled here, but bear in mind that with the rudder blade partly raised it will become harder to steer the boat. Also note that with the centreboard half raised, the boat will make more leeway than normal, so be prepared for more sideways drift of the boat as you approach – see the Key Factors chapter on page 47. You may choose to plan your approach to take account of this extra leeway slip.

When the water is shallow enough, release the mainsheet and kicking strap, then step into the shallow water and recover the trolley.

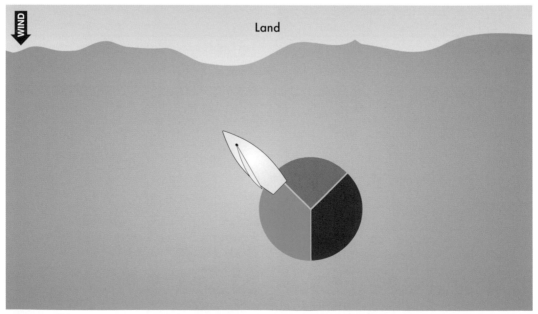

With an offshore wind, approach the beach ensuring you keep out of the no-go zone

COMMON MISTAKES

Launching

- Not understanding where the wind is blowing from: This would result in the boat being incorrectly positioned on the beach prior to hoisting the sails.
- Not parking the trolley above the high-water mark: This may result in it floating away if the tide comes in.
- Sailing away too fast before you have put the rudder down: The boat will be hard to control.

Recovery

- Approaching on a dead run point of sailing on a lee shore: This will mean that the boat will come in too fast and you will be unable to slow down.
- Not part lifting the rudder blade and centreboard when close to the shore: This will mean you will run aground before it is shallow enough to step ashore. You also risk damage to the foils.
- Not turning into the no-go zone as you step ashore: This could mean the boat will be hard to hold.

KEY LEARNING POINTS

Launching

- Establish what time high water is.
- Establish what direction the wind is blowing from by looking at flags, burgees or ripples on the water.
- Make sure your launching area is clear of obstacles or swimmers.
- In preparation for launching, park your boat on the beach with the bow pointing towards the wind, and hoist the sails.
- When you are ready to go, introduce the boat to the water, continuing to keep the bow pointing towards the wind.
- Return the trolley to the shore above the high-water seaweed mark.
- To avoid running aground whilst you sail away from the beach, lower just the tip of the rudder and centreboard.
- To sail away when the wind is onshore, use the close reach point of sailing.
- When the wind is cross shore, sail away on a beam reach.
- And when the wind is offshore, start on a beam reach and then turn to a training run.
- Sail out slowly until you are in deep water, turn back towards the no-go zone and lower the rudder.
- Lower the centreboard to suit your point of sailing.

Recovery

- Identify where the wind is coming from to allow you to determine how you will approach the shore.
- When the wind is blowing onshore, approach the beach on a broad reach point of sailing.
- When the wind is blowing cross shore, approach the beach on a beam reach point of sailing.
- When the wind is blowing offshore, approach the beach on a close-hauled point of sailing, being careful to keep clear of the no-go zone.
- Control your approach speed by releasing the mainsail so that it flaps.
- Part raise the rudder and centreboard to stop them hitting the bottom.
- To finally stop yourself when the water is shallow enough to stand up in, you should turn the boat deliberately into the no-go zone.
- Keep the boat pointing head to wind until the mainsail is lowered.

PONTOON
LAUNCHING
& RECOVERY

PONTOONS CAN MAKE LAUNCHING EASIER & KEEP YOUR FEET DRY

Go online for a video demonstration: www.fernhurstbooks.com – search for *Sailing: A Beginner's Guide* and click on 'Additional resources'.

Pontoons are large floating platforms that tend to be found in non-tidal locations and are usually situated on lakes or reservoirs. They are used for launching and are considerably easier to sail off from than a beach. What's more, you can usually manage to keep your feet dry.

FIRST STEPS

In preparation for launching, rig the mainsail, but do not hoist it, and hoist and furl the jib. In a Laser, rig the mast but do not connect the clew so as to allow the sail to flap in the wind.

Check for any obstructions on the slipway and look out for any slip or trip hazards that could arise during launch.

Check for slip hazards before launching

Ensure the bow of the boat is secured to the trolley with a painter.

Tie the boat to the trolley using the painter

If you have a lifting rudder, put it in place with the blade raised and make sure the safety clip is fitted. This prevents the rudder from falling off in the event of capsizing.

Fit the rudder

Ensure the safety clip is fitted

Next, position your trolley near the top of the gangway to the water. Check all the drainage bungs are in place on the back of the boat.

Boat preparing to launch and use a pontoon

ESTABLISH THE LEEWARD SIDE

The side of the pontoon that you must use is the leeward side. This is the side opposite to where the wind is blowing from. Use flags or other wind indicators to help you spot this. There could also be other boats already on the pontoon.

When secured to the leeward side, the boat will lie in the same direction as the wind and be held firmly in the middle of the no-go zone. This will mean that the sails will be easy to rig as they will flap when hoisted.

When the wind is blowing parallel to the pontoon, you can position your boat on either side.

Here the wind is blowing away from the camera, so the boats are using the end and far side of the pontoon

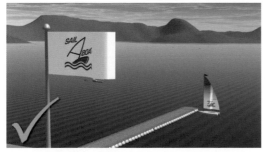

Only use the leeward side of the pontoon

Secure the bow of the boat to the pontoon with the painter

When the wind is blowing parallel to the pontoon, you can use either side

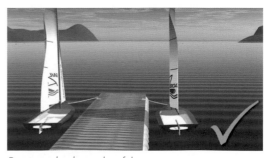

Boats tied either side of the pontoon

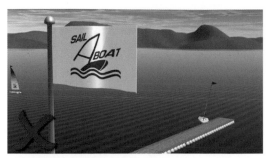

Never use the windward side of the pontoon

Do not secure the boat to the windward side of the pontoon as the location to hoist the sails. This makes rigging difficult and may cause damage or injury

TOP TIP

Do not try to use the windward side of the pontoon because the wind will force the boat against the pontoon during the rigging of the sails. This can cause damage to the boat or cause you injury by trapping your fingers and hands between the boat and the pontoon.

PONTOON LAUNCHING

Lower your boat down the slipway into the water, being careful not to slip. If the boat is heavy, ask for assistance.

When the boat and trolley are in the water the boat will float off the trolley. Untie the painter from the trolley and push the boat away, making sure that you keep hold of the painter!

Ask a friend to park the trolley in the dinghy

park. Next, walk the boat to the leeward side of the pontoon.

Secure the boat to the pontoon with the painter using a suitable knot. This will vary depending on the actual fixing on the pontoon but could be either a round turn and two half hitches or a figure-of-eight around the cleat (for more information on how to tie these knots see page 163).

Back at the boat, pull the boat towards you, being careful not to trap your fingers between the boat and the pontoon. You can then gently step aboard.

When stepping aboard, be sure to step as close to the centreline of the boat as possible.

Do not tread on the side tanks of the boat as, without the centreboard down, the boat is unstable and there would be a good chance of going for an embarrassing swim before you had even left the pontoon!

Push the centreboard down fully to increase stability as you move around the boat.

TOP TIP

Use a painter fixed to the bow of the boat to help manoeuvre the boat to the right position on the pontoon.

Use the painter to help manoeuvre the boat

Lower the boat down the slipway

Push the boat off (holding the painter!) and park the trolley

Walk the boat to the correct position on the leeward side of the pontoon

Tie the painter to the pontoon. A suitable knot to the pontoon is a round turn and two half hitches

Step aboard gently

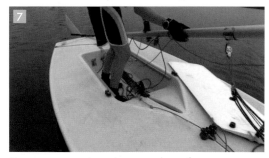

Keep your weight in the centreline of the boat

Do not step on the side of the boat

Insert or lower the centreboard

TOP TIP

When you climb on board, take the tail of the painter and secure it somewhere you can reach it. This makes it easier when you need to finally depart.

SINGLE-PERSON DINGHY

- Attach the clew of the sail to the boom and then tighten the kicking strap slightly
- Next, lower the rudder blade and climb back onto the pontoon to untie the painter
- Take a good look around to make sure that there are no other vessels in the immediate area
- Assuming it is clear, you are ready to depart
- Still standing on the pontoon, pick up the tiller extension and push the bow of the boat clear of the no-go zone whilst smartly stepping aboard, taking the painter with you
- Pull in the mainsheet to sail away and tidy up the painter so it doesn't fall over the side

Attach the clew of the sail to the boom

Ensure a tie down is used to keep the sail in close contact with the boom

Take all slack out of the kicking strap

Lower the rudder blade fully

The boat is now ready to leave

Get on the pontoon and untie the painter

Check the area is clear

Pick up the tiller extension and push the bow away from the pontoon and the no-go zone

Once aboard, pull the sail in and sail away

TWO-PERSON DINGHY

With the boat launched and secured to the pontoon and centreboard lowered:

- Hoist the mainsail, making sure the mainsheet is slack
- It is a good idea for the crew to help by feeding the sail into the track on the mast if they can
- Next, lower the rudder and secure the downhaul rope to hold the blade in place
- Unfurl the jib by releasing the cleat and pulling on the jibsheet
- Ask the crew to untie the painter and walk the boat as close as possible to the end of the pontoon to make an easy exit
- Take a good look around to check that no other boats are about to depart or arrive at the pontoon
- The boat will still be in the centre of the no-go zone
- To sail away, ask the crew to push the bow out of the no-go zone onto a close reach
- He then gently steps aboard, bringing the painter with him, being careful to get his weight as close as possible to the centreline of the boat
- Pull in both sails and sail away

With the centreboard lowered, hoist the mainsail

The crew can help feed the luff of the sail into the mast track

Lower the rudder blade fully and secure the downhaul

Release the furling line and pull on the jibsheet

Jib fully unfurled

Untie the painter in preparation for leaving

Take a good look around to check the area is clear

Push the boat onto a close reach point of sailing

Gently step aboard, keeping weight close to the centreline

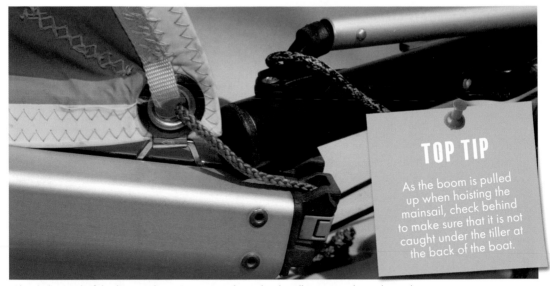

TOP TIP

As the boom is pulled up when hoisting the mainsail, check behind to make sure that it is not caught under the tiller at the back of the boat.

Check the end of the boom doesn't get caught under the tiller as you hoist the sail

PONTOON RECOVERY

This process is the same for both single-person and two-person dinghies. You MUST approach the pontoon from the leeward side, so read your masthead burgee or look to see where other boats are tied up.

Approach the pontoon from the leeward side

Do not approach from the windward side as you will be unable to control your speed and you risk either damaging or capsizing your boat.

Do NOT use the windward side

Using the windward side can be hazardous and you risk capsizing

The most important thing to remember is to approach the pontoon slowly. This reduces any chance of damage if you get things wrong and just makes the whole approach easier. The best angle to approach is from the close reach point of sailing, as this will allow you to easily control your speed by releasing the sails and keeps you out of the no-go zone.

The best approach angle is the close reach point of sailing

In a two-person boat, either release the jib and let it flap, or furl the jib and sail in under the mainsail alone.

In a two-person boat you can either let jib flap to control speed or furl the jib and sail in on the mainsail alone

However, if you misjudge things don't worry; simply tack around, sail away and then come back for another go.

Back on the correct approach, when you are a couple of boat lengths away from the pontoon, release the mainsheet totally so the sail flaps and let the momentum of the boat carry it to the pontoon. The boom should be over the side of the boat away from the pontoon and you should easily be able to grab the pontoon and step ashore.

If you misjudge things, tack around and try again

An alternative approach is to sail in on a close reach, with the sails flapping on one tack, and then tack round and grab the pontoon on the other side of the boat. This technique will stop the boat much more quickly.

Pick up and keep hold of the painter and then step ashore, tying the painter to a suitable fixing on the pontoon.

The crew stops the boat and climbs ashore taking the painter with them

Approach on a close reach

Tack around to stop the boat

Grab the pontoon

Take the painter with you as you step ashore

TOP TIP

Before you get out of the boat, release the kicking strap. This will help prevent the boat from capsizing on the pontoon should a gust of wind suddenly appear.

With the boat secured to the pontoon, you can then deal with the mainsail.

In the case of a single-person Laser, release the clew of the sail from the boom and let the sail flap.

Release the clew from the outhaul

Or, if your boat has a halyard, lower the sail. Disconnect the halyard from the head of the sail and secure this to the wire shroud. Then roll up the mainsail from the head and place it in the bottom of the boat. This process helps prevent the sail from accidentally blowing over the side of the boat as you manoeuvre it ashore.

- Raise the centreboard but be careful moving about once the centreboard is raised, as the boat will be less stable.
- Lift the rudder blade and lock it to prevent it from dropping back down.

- Pull the boat closer to the pontoon and step ashore but, as with launching, do not step on the side tanks as you do so: step from the centreline to the pontoon.
- Manoeuvre the boat close to the slipway and float it onto the trolley.
- Once the boat is safely back on the trolley, make sure you tie the painter firmly to the trolley. This will prevent the boat slipping off as you drag it clear of the water.
- Also, watch your step here as the slipway can get very slippery.

Lower the mainsail if you have a halyard

Secure the halyard to the shroud

Roll up the mainsail from the head and store it in the bottom of the boat

Raise the centreboard

Raise the rudder fully

Step ashore carefully

Manoeuvre the boat back to the slipway

Float the boat onto the trolley and secure the bow with the painter

Lift the boat clear of the water

COMMON MISTAKES

Launching

- Trying to launch from the wrong side of the pontoon
- Tying an unsuitable knot to secure the boat to the pontoon
- Stepping on the side of the boat and not the centreline

Recovery

- Approaching the pontoon on the wrong side
- Approaching the pontoon too fast on the wrong point of sailing
- Treading on the side tanks to step ashore
- Tying an unsuitable knot to secure the boat to the pontoon

KEY LEARNING POINTS

Launching

- Understand where the wind is blowing from and how that affects where you need to position your boat on the pontoon.
- Only use the downwind or leeward side of the pontoon.
- Never use the windward side of the pontoon.
- Look out for slip or trip hazards on the slipway prior to launching.
- Secure the boat to the pontoon itself with a suitable knot.
- When stepping into the boat, make sure you are as close as you can be to the centreline.
- When manoeuvring your boat, be careful not to trap your fingers between the side of the boat and the pontoon.
- Sail away from the pontoon on a close reach point of sailing.

Recovery

- Approach the pontoon from a leeward side on a close reach or close-hauled point of sailing.
- Never approach on the windward side on a downwind point of sailing.
- Control your approach speed by making the sails flap.
- Go round again if you are not correctly positioned or going too fast.
- Secure the boat to the pontoon with a suitable non-slip knot.

YOUR FIRST SAIL

KEEP THINGS SIMPLE FOR YOUR FIRST SAIL, LEARNING HOW TO START & STOP IS YOUR FIRST OBJECTIVE AFLOAT

Go online for a video demonstration: www.fernhurstbooks.com – search for *Sailing: A Beginner's Guide* and click on 'Additional resources'.

In this chapter you will learn the fundamentals of how a boat works and prepare for your first sail.

In your first few sailing sessions you should limit your sailing to fair weather days where the wind is blowing less than 16mph or a force 3 on the Beaufort scale – see page 66. Do not be tempted to sail in strong winds until you have mastered the basics in lighter conditions.

For your first sail, your objective is to try to understand where the wind is blowing from, get a feel for how the boat starts and stops by adjusting the sails, learn how to steer the boat using the rudder and how to turn around.

Sailing boats are driven by the wind and understanding where the wind is blowing from is integral to everything that happens on board. You must develop a good awareness of wind direction at all times to allow you to position the sails correctly.

For more information on this read the Points of Sailing and Key Factors chapters on pages 37 and 47.

HOW TO STEER

Whether sailing a single-person or a two-person boat, the person steering is called the helmsman and he also controls the mainsheet.

The boat is steered by the rudder blade, the movement of which is controlled by an arm attached to the rudder called the tiller. This in turn is fitted with a tiller extension, which you should hold to steer the boat at all times to ensure you are sitting in the best position. If you hold the tiller itself, you will be sitting too far back and this will upset the waterline of the boat, making it harder to steer.

Holding the tiller means you sit too far back

For your first sail, pick a day with gentle winds

Sitting well forward with the tiller extension across and in front of your body, you will gain good control and a feel for steering. Your other hand is free to hold the rope that pulls the mainsail in. This position is called the dagger grip.

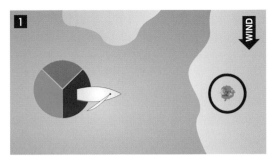

Taking a fixed landmark reduces the chance of becoming disorientated

Sit forward, holding the tiller in a dagger grip in your aft hand and the mainsheet in your fore hand

Keep referring to the landmark to stay on course

To steer the boat, gently push and pull the tiller extension in small amounts and always return the tiller to the central position to keep yourself sailing in a straight line. Remember that the boat will turn with even the smallest amount of movement on the rudder:

- Pushing the tiller towards the boom will turn the nose or bow of the boat towards the direction of the wind – this is called **luffing up**
- Pulling the tiller away from the boom will make the bow of the boat turn away from the wind – this is called **bearing away**

When sailing, it is a good idea to take note of fixed landmarks. This will give you a target to steer towards and help prevent you from becoming disorientated as you move about in the boat and the boat turns around.

Keep the tiller straight to go in a straight line

HOW TO ADJUST THE SAILS

To help you understand how the wind powers the boat you should think of your sail as an engine and the mainsheet (and jibsheet) as your accelerator and brake combined:

- Pulling in on the mainsheet will pull in the sail, which makes it fill with wind. This in turn

Position the boat on a beam reach with the sails flapping

generates drive to push the boat through the water.

- Letting the mainsheet go makes the sail flap, which reduces power and subsequently slows you down.

To understand how the wind interacts with the boat, it is best to start from the beam reach point of sailing. A beam reach is where the wind blows at right angles to the direction the boat is pointing. This is the easiest point of sailing to understand as the boat is well clear of the no-go zone. Refer to the Points of Sailing chapter on page 37 for more information on this.

Starting with the control sheets loose and the sails flapping, make sure the tiller is central. Next gently pull the control sheets until the sails don't flap any more.

You will notice that the boat will immediately drive forwards. When you pull a sail in from a slack position, the last bit to fill with wind is the front part of the sail. So this is the area to look at to make sure that it doesn't flap.

Sailing dinghies don't have brakes, so to slow down you must release the power in the sails by letting out the control sheets until the sails flap.

Gently pull the mainsheet to make the boat move forwards

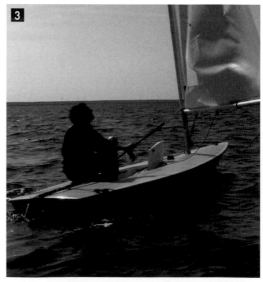

To stop, release the mainsheet so the sail flaps

You should practise releasing and tightening the sails to get a feel for how the boat accelerates and slows down.

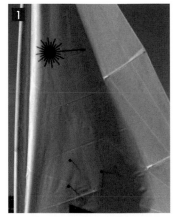
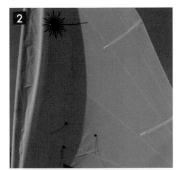

Look for the point where the sail starts to flap

Pull the mainsheet in to stop the sail flapping

Continue pulling until the sail doesn't flap

With the sails trimmed correctly the boat moves forward

107

TURNING AROUND

For your first sail, when you need to turn around you should use the tacking manoeuvre. For a detailed explanation of this read the How to Tack chapter on page 113. But to start with, the basic steps of tacking are:

- First take a good look around to check the turning area is clear
- If so, inform the crew that you intend to start the manoeuvre, if sailing a two-person boat
- Then PUSH the tiller towards the boom and release the mainsheet

- The boat will immediately turn
- Duck under the boom and move onto the new side of the boat
- If in a two-person boat, get the crew to release the jibsheet and pull the jib across
- Continue turning until the boat has gone round through 180° and you are facing the direction from which you have just sailed
- Then straighten the tiller and swap your hands over
- Adjust the sail control sheets to find the point where the sails don't flap

To turn around, gently push the tiller towards the boom

The boat will immediately turn; prepare to duck

Move to the centreline and duck as the boom moves across

Continue turning until you point back to where you have just come from

Straighten the tiller and move onto the side

Swap your hands and sail away

STUCK IN IRONS

Whilst tacking across the wind, you may straighten the rudder too soon. If you do, you will be stuck in the no-go zone with the bow of the boat pointing head to wind. This is called being stuck in irons and you will be unable to sail.

Push the boom and tiller out on the same side to force the boat backwards

As the boat moves backwards and turns, continue to push out both the boom and tiller

The boat is in the middle of the no-go zone and stuck in irons

If this happens, don't worry. You need to force the bow of the boat to one side of the no-go zone or the other.

To achieve this in a single-person boat, push the mainsail out by hand as far as you can with the boom. At the same time push the tiller towards the boom. This will force the wind to hit the back of the sail, which will introduce drive and start to push you backwards, turning the boat clear of the no-go zone.

Once the boat has turned well clear of the no-go zone, you can then release the boom, quickly straighten the tiller and pull in the mainsheet to sail away.

In short, it's:
- A push on the boom
- And a push on the tiller
- Followed by a pull on the mainsheet
- And a pull on the tiller

When the boat has turned 90°, let go of the boom and pull on the mainsheet; pull the tiller back to the centre and sail off

In a two-person dinghy, things are a little easier. If you get stuck in the no-go zone, simply ask the crew to hold the clew of the jib as far out to one side as he can.

The leverage of the wind on the back side of the jib will force the boat out of the no-go zone, at which point let the jib go, pull it back across and then sail away.

When a two-person boat is stuck in irons, release the mainsheet

The crew pulls the jib to one side

The boat will turn

After the boat turns through 90°, release the jib and pull across, pulling in the mainsail at the same time

HOW TO STOP & TAKE A REST

If you want to stop and have a rest for a while in a two-person boat, adopt the hove-to position. In a single-person dinghy this is called lying to.

In a single-person boat, bring the boat onto a close reach point of sailing and release the mainsheet so it flaps. Free off the kicking strap so it is slack, and part raise the centreboard. Maintain this heading, keeping the boom out to the side.

In a two-person boat, again position the boat on the close reach point of sailing. Ask the crew to pull the jib across onto the wrong (i.e. windward) side of the boat and release the mainsail so it flaps. Free off the kicking strap and half raise the centreboard. Push the tiller towards the boom, and the boat will almost stop.

Single-person boat lying to

To get going again in a single-person boat, simply pull in the mainsail and tighten the kicking strap slightly.

On a two-person boat, release the jib and pull it across to the leeward side of the boat. Pull in the mainsheet and kicking strap and straighten the tiller to sail away.

Two-person boat hove-to

WINDIER WEATHER

If you sail in windier conditions, the procedures are the same, but they happen much faster. You will notice that the boat will turn more quickly, the sails will flap more loudly, and the boom will travel across the boat faster.

You should consider reefing the mainsail on windy days – this reduces the amount of sail area and takes some of the power away. Read the Reefing chapter on page 169 to see how to reef the sails.

COMMON MISTAKES
- Not understanding where the wind is blowing from, so not setting the sails correctly for the point of sailing you are on. See the Points of Sailing chapter on page 37 for more information.
- Getting stuck in irons due to straightening the tiller before you have passed through the no-go zone when tacking.
- Not keeping a good lookout can put you in a hazardous area with lots of boats or other water users.

KEY LEARNING POINTS
- First time out, avoid winds greater than about 15 miles per hour so that you can practise manoeuvring at manageable speeds.
- Pulling in the mainsheet so that the mainsail fills with wind will drive your boat forward.
- Releasing the mainsheet so that the mainsail flaps in the wind will lose drive and slow you down.
- In your early days of sailing, the easiest condition to practise in is when the wind is blowing across the boat at 90°. This is called a beam reach.
- The safest way to turn your boat around is to tack, which is when the bow or nose of the boat goes through the eye of the wind (no-go zone) and out onto the other side.
- It's likely that you will become disorientated as you tack back and forth, so before you turn identify a landmark to aim at which will become a reference point for you.
- If you get stuck in the no-go zone, in a single-person boat push the boom away from you and push the tiller towards the boom. When the mainsail then fills with wind, pull the tiller towards you again, pull the sail in and sail away. In a two-person boat, back the jib.

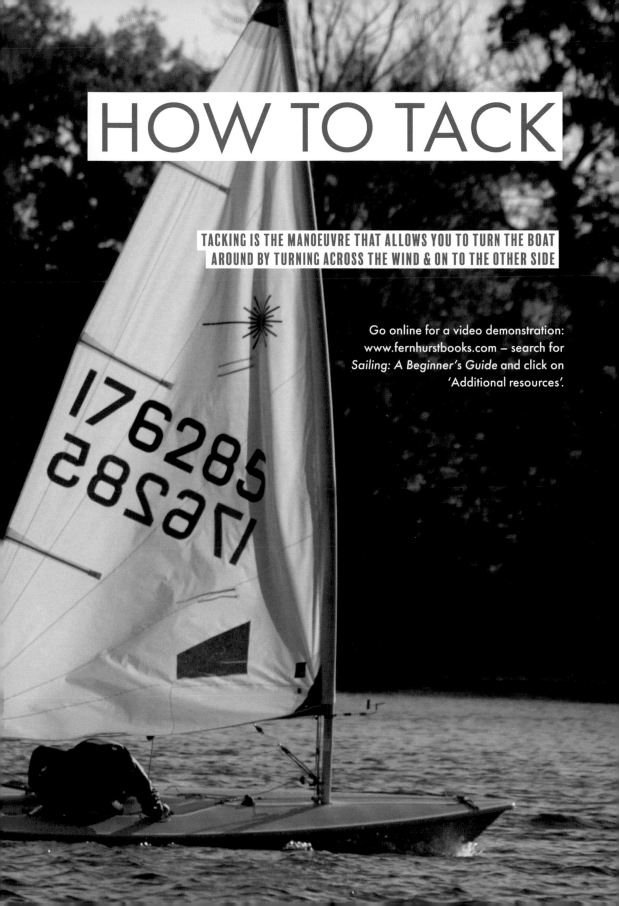

HOW TO TACK

TACKING IS THE MANOEUVRE THAT ALLOWS YOU TO TURN THE BOAT AROUND BY TURNING ACROSS THE WIND & ON TO THE OTHER SIDE

Go online for a video demonstration: www.fernhurstbooks.com – search for *Sailing: A Beginner's Guide* and click on 'Additional resources'.

In this chapter you will learn how to tack a dinghy.

Tacking is the manoeuvre that allows you to turn the boat around by turning the bow of the boat through the wind / no-go zone.

Tacking takes the boat from one side of the no-go zone to the other

You can start to tack from any point of sailing and turn to any point of sailing on the opposite tack.

This chapter will focus on starting from the close-hauled point of sailing on one side, turning the boat through the no-go zone and then on to the close-hauled point of sailing on the other tack. (Refer to the Points of Sailing chapter on page 37 for more information on this).

As previously mentioned in the book, the wind has a zone of about 45° either side of where it's blowing from in which you can't sail. This is called the no-go zone and here the sails won't work.

When tacking, the boat will turn from one side of the no-go zone to the other and the sails will flap. This reduces drive and slows the boat down. When turning, it is best to master tacking before attempting the alternative, faster manoeuvre called gybing, which is the subject of another chapter on page 123.

The basic principles for tacking are the same for the helmsman, whether sailing a single-person or two-person dinghy.

● ●
SAFETY POINT
You should only tack if your sailing area is clear from other vessels or obstructions. To do this, you should take a good look around, over both shoulders and behind you, to check that the area is clear. If not, you should wait until it is clear or slow down to let the other vessel pass.
● ●

Start the manoeuvre from the close-hauled point of sailing

During the tack the bow of the boat turns across the wind, through the no-go zone

The tack is completed once the opposite close-hauled point of sailing is reached

By combining a series of tacks together with maintaining the close-hauled point of sailing, it is possible to sail your boat towards the direction the wind is blowing from, and this is called beating.

ESTABLISH A CLOSE-HAULED POINT OF SAILING

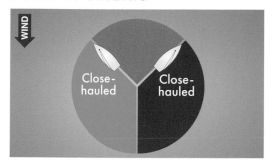

The close-hauled point of sailing is on the edge of the no-go zone

Firstly, establish yourself on the close-hauled point of sailing. To do this, pull in the sails hard so the boom ends up over the leeward corner of the boat. Hold the tip of the tiller extension across and in front of your body, with your thumb pointing towards the end of the tiller extension and hold the mainsheet in the other hand. This is called the dagger grip and it allows you to easily steer the boat with one hand and be ready to adjust or release the mainsheet with the other if a gust of wind hits you and the boat heels over.

The helmsman holds the tiller extension in a dagger grip in their back hand and the mainsheet in their front hand

Push the centreboard fully down and, in the case of a two-person dinghy, ask the crew to pull the jib in hard.

Next, gently push the tiller towards the boom. This will turn the boat towards the wind, which is called 'luffing up'. Continue to turn gently until you

see the front edge of the sail start to 'back' – this is where the sail starts to fill with wind from the other side.

When this point is reached, gently pull the tiller away from the boom until the sail snaps into an even shape and then straighten the tiller. This is called 'bearing away'.

On a two-person boat, look at the front edge of the jib to find the edge of the no-go zone: when it starts lifting

Bear away slightly and the jib 'pops' into shape

On a single-person dinghy look at the front edge of the mainsail and watch for when that starts to lift.

As you get more proficient you should be able to adjust the steering of the boat by very small amounts, paying attention to the telltales, which will react before the sail will 'back' (see page 51).

You are now on the close-hauled point of sailing and on the edge of the no-go zone.

To maintain the close-hauled point of sailing, continually repeat the action of gently luffing up and bearing away by pushing and pulling the tiller towards and away from the boom in very small amounts whilst looking for the point where the sail starts to back.

TOP TIP

Apply small, gentle tiller movements. Pushing the tiller too fast and hard here will put you in the middle of the no-go zone where you will either stop or tack accidentally.

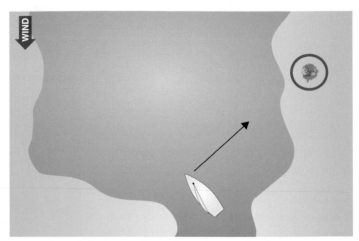

During the tack the boat will turn through 90°. Identify a new target destination before you start

SINGLE-PERSON DINGHY

Let's look first at how to tack a single-person dinghy.

Establish the boat on the close-hauled point of sailing and check the area is clear of hazards.

It is important to check over both shoulders and look under the boom to see if there are any immediate hazards. Sailing in a single-person dinghy calls for extra vigilance as there is no crew to assist you. Do not tack if by doing so you will be turning directly into the path of an oncoming boat. It is best to wait until they have passed before tacking. An exception to this would be when two boats are directly converging. See the Rules of the Road chapter (page 177) for more information on this.

- Prepare to step across the boat by leading with your back foot. This will ensure that you face forward during the manoeuvre.
- After this, release about one metre of mainsheet to slow the boat down, making it easier to get under the boom.
- Gently push the tiller towards the boom.
- As soon as the tiller is pushed, the boat will immediately start to turn into the no-go zone and the sails will begin to flap.

- As the boom moves across the boat, duck under the boom and step across the boat.
- Keep your head down here to avoid being hit by the boom.
- Keep the tiller pushed over to allow the boat to continue to turn through the no-go zone and onto the close-hauled point of sailing on the opposite tack.
- Don't worry if the sails flap noisily during the turn – this is normal.
- When the boom has flipped across and moved over to the opposite side of the boat, sit down on the new windward side (i.e. the side closest to the wind) as far forward as you can.
- Next, locate the new landmark or target you selected before the turn and ensure you end up pointing towards this mark.
- Straighten the tiller, still holding the extension behind your back. (This will feel a little odd to start with but it is possible to steer the boat like this for some distance.)
- Changing hands is easier if you are seated and there is less chance of dropping the tiller, which will make the boat turn out of control.

SWAP HANDS

Next, you should swap hands by taking the hand holding the mainsheet to the tiller extension behind your back. To make things easier, ensure your new hand has the thumb pointing towards the end of the tiller extension. This avoids an awkward twist of the wrist in the next step.

Then let go of the tiller extension with the original hand and rotate the extension under your arm – you may need to lean forwards towards the bow slightly here.

Finally, position the tiller extension back in front of your body and grab the mainsheet with your front hand, resuming the dagger grip.

Pull in the mainsheet once more and probe the tiller to find the close-hauled point of sailing on the edge of the no-go zone.

TOP TIP

Hold the tiller extension as close to the end as you can – this provides greater control and makes things easier later on in the tack.

Take a good look around

Release one metre of mainsheet

Push the tiller extension towards the boom gently

As the boat turns, duck under the boom as it moves across and change sides

Sit on the new side with your weight well forward – the hands haven't swapped yet

Prepare to swap hands

Take the old mainsheet hand back to the tiller extension; point the thumbs on both hands together

Release the original (now front) hand, lean forward and roll the tiller extension under your arm

Resume the dagger grip on the tiller, pull in the mainsheet and establish a close-hauled point of sailing

TOP TIP

Look to find the landmark you picked before the turn as this will help you to judge if you have turned the correct amount.

Two person dinghy tacking

TWO-PERSON DINGHY

Let's now look at how to tack a two-person dinghy. As mentioned, there are many similarities for the helmsman between tacking a two-person or a single-person dinghy, but the second person complicates things slightly.

Sailing a two-person dinghy requires teamwork and good communication as it relies on both helm and crew working together. The helmsman must not tack if the crew is not ready.

The helmsman establishes the boat on the close-hauled point of sailing and checks the immediate areas for hazards and other vessels. He only proceeds if it is clear.

The first step for the helmsman is to shout 'ready about'. This is the command to inform the crew that

the manoeuvre is imminent.

The crew should then also check for hazards and other vessels and, if it is clear, release the jibsheet from any jam cleat, keeping hold of the jibsheet and replying 'all clear'. The helmsman must hear this response before proceeding.

The helmsman prepares to step across the boat leading with his back foot. This ensures that he faces forward during the manoeuvre.

To make the tack simpler, the helmsman releases about one metre of mainsheet. This slows the boat down and makes it easier to get under the boom.

Next the helmsman shouts 'lee oh'. This is the command to tell the crew that the tack is about to start.

At the same time he gently pushes the tiller towards the boom and both people prepare to duck. The boat will immediately start to turn and enter the no-go zone. The boom will begin to swing towards the centre of the boat and the sails will flap.

The crew should release the jibsheet to let the jib flap.

As the boom reaches the centreline of the boat, both helm and crew duck under the boom and step across the boat. They keep their heads down here to avoid being hit by the travelling boom.

Once the boom has moved over to the new leeward side of the boat (i.e. the side furthest from the wind), both helm and crew should sit down on the opposite side as far forward as they can, with the tiller extension still behind the helmsman's back. The helm continues to turn the boat until he has located the new landmark or target selected before the tack. He then straightens the tiller.

The crew, meanwhile, pulls the jib in hard and secures the jibsheet in the appropriate jam cleat if the boat has one.

SWAP HANDS

Next, the helmsman should swap hands (as detailed for the single-person boat).

Once the helmsman has swapped his hands over, both sails are pulled in tight again and the helmsman probes the tiller to find the close-hauled point of sailing once more, i.e. the point where the sail is not flapping.

After checking the area is clear the helmsman shouts 'ready about' while the crew prepares to release the jibsheet and confirms 'all clear'

The helmsman shouts 'lee oh' and releases about one metre of mainsheet while the crew frees the jibsheet out of the cleat

The helmsman gently pushes the tiller extension towards the boom and the boat turns immediately

As it turns, the helm and crew duck well under the moving boom while the sails flap and cross sides

The helm and crew sit on the new side and the crew pulls the jibsheet tight

The helmsman swaps hands by taking the old mainsheet hand (now aft) to the tiller extension with both thumbs pointing together

He releases the tiller extension from the old hand, leans forward and rolls the tiller extension under his arm

He resumes the dagger grip of the tiller with his aft hand once more and pulls in the mainsheet with his front hand

NEXT STEPS

Practise tacking slowly to start with. Speed comes later. Bad habits will be formed which will be hard to break unless you do things slowly to begin with.

You can even practise on dry land first. Place some old tyres under the back of the boat – there's no need to hoist the sails – tie the boom up using the halyard fixed to the outhaul at the end of the boom. Climb into the boat and ask a friend to mimic the wind by pushing the boom across the boat.

First time out on the water, avoid winds greater than about 12 miles an hour so that you can carry out the manoeuvre at a manageable speed.

Practise sailing as close to the no-go zone as you can, until the front edge of the headsail doesn't flap, and then start tacking.

Keep tacking from one side of the no-go zone to the other until you feel comfortable with all the steps.

Practise your skills ashore with a land drill

When performing a tack ensure you keep well clear of other vessels during the manoeuvre

COMMON MISTAKES

- Not starting the manoeuvre from the close-hauled point of sailing. If you are not close-hauled, you will not make any headway towards the wind – you will simply go backwards and forwards along the same line. So ensure that you are sailing close-hauled.
- Pushing the tiller across too hard during the tack. There is a risk you will turn the boat too quickly and you may not be able to get across the boat in time before you capsize.
- Failure to straighten the rudder after the manoeuvre will allow the boat to continue to turn and you could well end up doing a complete 360° turn.
- Forgetting to duck under the boom. You may consider wearing a hard hat similar to a canoeist helmet. This is particularly advisable for children.
- Straightening the rudder too soon when you are still in the no-go zone. This will stop the boat with no drive in the sail and you will find yourself completely stuck in irons – see page 109.

KEY LEARNING POINTS

- Tacking is the manoeuvre that allows you to turn the boat around from any point of sailing by turning the bow of the boat through the eye of the wind (no-go zone).
- The wind has a zone of about 45° either side of where it's blowing from in which you can't sail. This is called the no-go zone and a boat turns through this zone when tacking.
- The boat slows significantly during the turn when tacking, so it is best to learn this manoeuvre before attempting the faster way of turning called the gybe (see page 123).
- A series of tacks combined with the close-hauled point of sailing is called beating and allows you to sail towards the wind.
- When sailing towards the wind you should be on a close-hauled point of sailing, with the sails pulled in hard and not flapping.
- Ensure you use small tiller movements when steering rather than large ones.
- Identify a new landmark or target point before you start your tack to stop you getting disorientated.
- Check the area is free from obstructions and only tack if it is clear.
- Good communications between helm and crew are vital.
- Effective grip and hand-swapping techniques with the tiller and control sheets are among the key factors to successful tacking.
- Release about one metre of mainsheet before you tack to slow the boat down and make it easier to get under the boom.
- Lead with your back foot to ensure that you face forward throughout the manoeuvre.

HOW TO GYBE

GYBING IS THE MANOEUVRE THAT ALLOWS THE BOAT TO TURN ACROSS THE WIND WHEN SAILING DOWNWIND. OFTEN THE SUBJECT OF AN UNWELCOME CAPSIZE

Go online for a video demonstration: www.fernhurstbooks.com – search for *Sailing: A Beginner's Guide* and click on 'Additional resources'.

In this chapter you will learn the steps of how to gybe your dinghy. Gybing is the manoeuvre that allows you to change direction by turning the stern of the boat through the wind when you are on a reaching or running point of sailing (see the Points of Sailing chapter on page 37).

Unlike the tacking manoeuvre where the bow of the boat turns through the wind, causing the sails

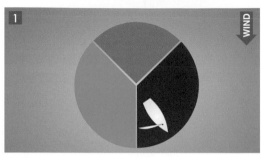

Start on a training run

to flap and the boat to lose power and speed, during the gybe the bow of the boat is pointing away from the wind, so the rig is under power at all times.

The boom will travel a long distance under load and this can be fast. Gybing is often the cause of an unwelcome capsize.

That said, gybing is nothing to fear and is easy to master. Good balance technique is a key factor.

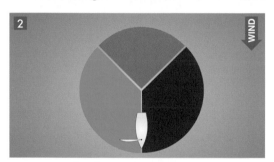

Turn onto a dead run

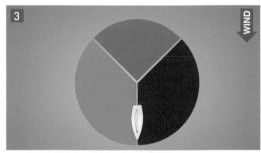

The wind gets behind the sail and flicks it across

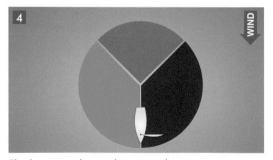

The boom settles on the new side

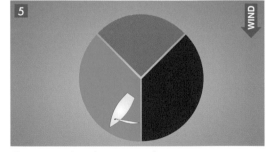

Once completed you can adjust your course

SAFETY POINT

Don't gybe if your sailing area is not clear. Take a good look around, particularly under the boom and in front of the boat as this is the direction of travel during the manoeuvre. Also check behind your back for approaching vessels. If there is any doubt, wait until the area is clear.

Be careful of the moving boom, which can flick across the boat very fast. Duck well clear of it.

On a windy day the gybe will happen very fast, and the helm and crew must be prepared to move their weight extremely quickly to the new side of the boat to avoid an unwelcome capsize.

Check the area under the boom is clear

The direction of travel is ahead and under the boom

ESTABLISHING A TRAINING RUN

The basic steps taken by the helmsman are the same, whether sailing a single-person or two-person boat. In the two-person boat the crew adds an extra element of communication.

You can gybe from any downwind point of sailing to any other downwind point of sailing on the opposite side, but it is best to learn by gybing between training runs on opposite sides.

A training run is when the boat is sailing approximately 150° off the wind (for more information see the Points of Sailing chapter on page 37).

The boom should be well out to the side of the boat and the centreboard should be about three-quarters up.

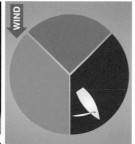

Lift the daggerboard so it is about three-quarters raised

Establishing a training run

Or with a centreboard that pivots around a pin, have it about three-quarters raised

On a training run there is less chance of the wind accidentally flicking the boom across before you are ready to turn.

From a training run the turning angle for the completed manoeuvre will only be about 60°.

The direction of travel that the boat will make during the gybe is towards the leeward bow side of the boat. This is in front and under the sail and is the area you must check to see that it is clear from any hazards before attempting to gybe.

To prevent becoming disorientated during the manoeuvre, identify a likely new transit point before you turn.

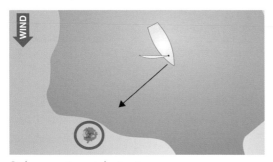

Pick a new target destination

In both single- and two-person boats, during the gybe the boom will flick across the boat extremely quickly from one side to the other. The whole manoeuvre can take less than a second! It is therefore vital to duck down low to avoid being hit by the boom.

Make sure you duck well clear of the moving boom

You must also be prepared to move your weight extremely quickly across to the new windward side to balance the boat. The force of the boom can easily capsize the boat, particularly if the wind is strong.

Be prepared to quickly balance the boat once the boom has moved across

To reduce the amount of travel of the boom, you should first pull in the mainsheet by a couple of metres. This will make the whole manoeuvre a little safer while you are learning.

WHEN IS THE SAIL READY TO MOVE ACROSS?

Understanding when the boom is ready to move across is an important skill to learn for both single-person and two-person boats.

The point you are looking for is when the pressure in the mainsheet becomes momentarily light. This lasts for a very short period of time and indicates the moment when the wind is changing sides on the sail.

When you feel this point, you should yank the mainsheet sharply to force the boom across. Depending on your mainsheet configuration, you either pull the mainsheet falls across or tug in the mainsheet.

When the weight in the mainsheet feels neutral, pull the boom across

On a single-person boat, sharply pull the mainsheet when the weight feels light

In doing this, you dictate the point when the boat actually gybes and this helps you to maintain control and know when to balance the boat. If sailing a Laser, it will also help prevent the mainsheet from becoming snagged on the end of the transom.

Some dinghies, like the Laser, are prone to the mainsheet snagging the transom during the gybe

If you do not force the boom across, then the wind will do this for you, which may catch you unprepared. The impact is such that you are likely to capsize. Also, the turning angle for the manoeuvre will increase.

SINGLE-PERSON DINGHY

Establish the training run, with centreboard about three-quarters up, and sit on the windward side of the boat, holding the tiller extension in the dagger grip.

- Check under the boom that the area is clear
- If so, pull in some mainsheet
- Keeping the tiller straight, roll the tiller extension so the tip points towards the boom
- Shift your weight closer to the centreline of the boat
- Have one final look around and gently push the tiller away from the boom and duck
- The boat will turn immediately and quickly, so keep the tiller movement small
- As the boat turns, feel for the weightless point in the mainsheet and give it a tug to force the boom across
- The boom will then flick from one side of the boat to the other
- When you feel the boom move across the boat, you must balance the boat and then immediately straighten the tiller as the boom settles on the new side
- If you do not do this, the boat will continue to turn and there is a chance you will spin round in a full circle
- Note that the tiller extension should now be behind your back

SWAP HANDS

- Take the hand that is holding the mainsheet back to the tiller extension and grab it with your thumb pointing towards the end
- Let go with your original hand, lean forward slightly and roll the tiller extension under your arm
- Resume the dagger grip once more, grabbing the mainsheet with your front hand

The final step is to ease the mainsheet back out a little bit to suit the training run and sail away.

Pull in some mainsheet to restrict boom movement

Rotate the tiller extension so the tip points towards the boom

Duck under the moving boom

As the boom settles, straighten the tiller immediately

Lean forward and roll the tiller extension under your arm

Resume the dagger grip and continue sailing

Push the tiller away from the boom to start the turn

When the mainsheet feels light, yank the mainsheet hard to force the boom to flick across the boat

Sit well forward and prepare to swap hands

Point the thumbs together

TWO-PERSON DINGHY

As mentioned, there are many similarities with the actions of the helmsman, whether sailing a single-person or two-person dinghy. With a two-person boat, good communication between helm and crew is vital, particularly as the boom can move across quickly and it is common for the crew to hit his head on the boom if he doesn't know the gybe is happening.

The helmsman establishes the training run with the tiller in the dagger grip and mainsheet eased so the boom is almost 90° over the side of the boat. The centreboard is about three-quarters up.

His new sailing direction will be towards a point under the boom in front of the boat, so he needs to check this area is clear from hazards or obstructions. Bearing in mind that these are likely to be hidden by the jib, it is very important to look under this sail. This will also help prevent the helmsman from becoming disorientated during

the manoeuvre. Before turning, he should look behind his back as well, as other vessels may be approaching from that angle.

To alert the crew that the gybe is imminent the helmsman shouts 'standby to gybe'.

The crew then double checks the area is clear, making sure his feet are not caught in any trailing ropes. He releases the jibsheet from the jam cleat in one hand and picks up the new jibsheet in the other. The crew then replies 'all clear'.

The helmsman must not proceed without this return communication from the crew.

The helm then pulls the mainsheet in by a couple of metres to restrict the travel of the boom and, keeping the tiller straight, rolls the tiller extension over the top of the tiller so the tip points towards the boom.

He moves his weight close to the centreline of the boat, leading with his back foot first. This will ensure that he is facing in the right direction during the turn.

129

Next, he shouts 'gybe oh', at which point both he and the crew should duck. The helm then gently pushes the tiller away from the boom and the boat turns immediately. He must not push the tiller hard across as this can make the turn too fast. It is best not to push the tiller more than 45° for a controlled turn.

The helm grabs hold of the mainsheet falls and when these feel light, he pulls the boom across.

Both helm and crew keep their heads well out of the way of the rapidly moving boom and move across to the other side quickly to balance the boat.

Once the boom has settled, the helm immediately straightens the tiller to stop the boat turning any further and sits down as far forward as he can. Next, swap hands as described in the single-person section in this chapter.

The helmsman establishes a training run

The helmsman and crew check the turning area is clear

After pulling in the mainsheet slightly, the helm rolls the tiller extension to point towards the boom, but keeps the tiller straight

The helmsman moves to the centre of the boat and keeps the tiller straight

He gently pushes the tiller away from the boom to start the turn, avoiding excessive tiller movement

When the mainsheet feels light, the helmsman grabs the mainsheet falls and pulls them across

They both duck under the boom as it crosses the boat

The helmsman straightens the tiller immediately the boom has settled, sits down and prepares to swap hands

Having swapped hands, the helmsman releases the mainsheet to allow the boom to move out and sails away

NEXT STEPS

Practise gybing as often as you can. Remember that the stronger the wind, the faster and potentially more hazardous this manoeuvre can be.

You can even practise on dry land first. With the boat on its trolley, support the stern of the boat with some old tyres. There is no need to hoist the sails, simply tie the boom up using the main halyard or another suitable rope from the outer end to the mast. Ask a friend to mimic the wind by pushing and pulling the boom across, while you do the manoeuvres in the boat.

For your first time out, avoid gybing in strong winds as it is likely the boat will capsize. If you are concerned about the wind strength and you need to get to a direction on the opposite downwind point of sailing, you can always tack round rather than gybe (see How to Tack chapter on page 113). This takes the boat the long way round but will avoid an unwelcome capsize.

Practise onshore with a land drill

COMMON MISTAKES

- Not being on a training run to start the gybe. This means it is harder to identify the point when the boom is ready to flick across to the other side of the boat.
- Pushing the tiller towards the boom. This will make the boat tack. In order to gybe, you must pull the tiller away from the boom.
- Not pulling in a couple of metres of mainsheet before the gybe. This will make the boom flick across wildly and could capsize the boat.
- Not moving your weight quickly enough to balance the boat once the boom flicks across. This also may capsize you.
- Not straightening the tiller immediately after the boom has gone across. You may end up sailing in a circle.
- Straightening the tiller before the boom has flicked across. You are likely to be on a dead run point of sailing and an accidental gybe could happen, again possibly causing the boat to capsize. Also, you will not have completed the manoeuvre.
- On a Laser, forgetting to pull the mainsheet in quickly as the boom is moving across. This will result in the mainsheet catching on the back of the boat and you will be unable to control the sail. If windy, you are likely to capsize.
- Failing to duck. The boom can travel a long way from side to side and can do so very quickly. This can cause a serious head injury if you get caught in the way.

KEY LEARNING POINTS

- A gybe is the manoeuvre to turn the boat when the boat is on a downwind point of sailing.
- You should start on a training run with the boom almost 90° out and the centreboard three-quarters up.
- Only gybe if the area is safe and clear.
- To reduce the travel the boom makes, pull the mainsail in a little before you start.
- As the boat turns, when the weight in the mainsheet feels light, pull the boom over to help maintain control.
- Straighten the tiller immediately the boom has gone across.
- Balance the boat quickly.
- Do not forget to duck.

CAPSIZE, RECOVERY & RESCUE

A CAPSIZE CAN OCCUR ON ANY POINT OF SAILING, USUALLY WHEN TOO MUCH WIND HITS THE BOAT

Go online for a video demonstration: www.fernhurstbooks.com – search for *Sailing: A Beginner's Guide* and click on 'Additional resources'.

Everyone capsizes

Capsizing is a normal part of everyday sailing. Even very experienced sailors capsize, and the most common cause is when the wind simply overpowers you and knocks you over. There is nothing to worry about when it happens, and the boat won't sink. Dinghies tend to have plenty of buoyancy built into the design, which prevents them from sinking, even if one of the buoyancy tanks becomes holed and knocks the boat over.

In time, the number of capsizes you have will reduce, but a practised capsize drill will allow you to recover the boat easily.

With any capsize, the trick is to keep calm and apply a gentle, sustained pressure to the boat when you are trying to right it. If you panic and overexert yourself, you could injure yourself as well as tire yourself out quickly.

A common concern when starting out is what happens if you get caught under the sail in the water.

If this happens do not panic; your buoyancy aid will provide enough leverage for you to push the sail up. This will introduce a pocket of air under the sail so you can breathe and then simply swim free.

If caught under the sail, push up and swim free

Another concern is what happens if you get caught under the upturned hull should it invert. Boats turn from a capsized to an inverted position slowly, so there should be ample time to swim clear if you feel this is happening. However, if you do get caught under the boat, there should be a pocket of air. Simply take a big breath and swim out from under the upturned hull.

To prevent the boat from inverting should a capsize occur, you may prefer to fit a masthead flotation bag to the top of the mainsail, which adds buoyancy to the masthead. See page 32 for how to rig this.

Masthead flotation bags prevent the boat from inverting in the event of a capsize

SAFETY POINT

In some countries, even in mid-summer the water will be cold. If it is windy, it is a good idea to wear a wetsuit as this will help to keep you warm should you end up in the water. In winter months a drysuit is better still as this will keep you completely dry (see page 70).

Wetsuits are good if its windy, even in mid-summer

SINGLE-PERSON DINGHY

Single-person dinghies are lighter than two-person dinghies and, as such, are generally easier to pull back upright from a capsize.

When you end up in the water, make sure you are not tangled in any ropes and try to loosen the mainsheet totally.

It is important to keep in direct contact with the boat by either holding onto the hull or picking up the mainsheet.

Swim to the stern of the boat, taking the end of the mainsheet with you. This will stop you becoming separated from the boat and will also prevent you from becoming trapped under the hull should it invert. Check the rudder hasn't fallen off. If it has, refit it.

Before you go afloat always check the rudder has a retraining pin or clip to stop it slipping off if the boat capsizes.

If the boat has inverted, swim to the windward side and climb onto the upturned gunwale of the boat, using the centreboard for support. If it is pointing bow to wind, then either side will do.

Next, ensure that the centreboard is fully extended to provide greater leverage. Holding the centreboard, lean back whilst applying steady pressure on it. A gentle, steady force is the key here so there is no need to overexert yourself.

Gradually the boat will adopt the flat capsize position, i.e. lying on its side, flat on the water. When in this position, apply all your weight to the upper surface of the centreboard and push down. This will force the sail to pop out of the water. A sharp pump on the centreboard may be necessary to break the surface tension caused by the sail sticking to the water. Once the sail has become clear of the water, the boat will right itself quickly.

You should now be in the water next to the boat. Let the boom settle and prepare to climb back on board. Do not climb in under the boom as this might pull the boat back over again. Swim to the windward side so that the boom is lying away from you. You can grab hold of the toestraps to help pull yourself back into the boat.

When aboard, check that all the control lines are not tangled, open any drainage points, grab the tiller extension and pull the sail in to sail away.

Keep contact with the boat at all times

Climb onto the upturned lip (gunwale) of the boat by the centreboard

When the flat capsize position is reached, apply weight to the top of the centreboard

Swim to the windward side

Swim to the stern, taking the mainsheet with you

Check the rudder is still in place

Fully extend the centreboard to provide greater leverage

Lean back and apply constant weight to the centreboard

Keep pushing as the boat comes up

Keep hold of the boat when the boat is upright

Do not climb in under the boom

Pull on the toestraps for more leverage

Climb aboard

Tidy up loose ropes and sail away

DRY CAPSIZE

As you get more proficient and experienced, it is possible to right the boat without actually getting wet. This is called a dry capsize and here's how you do it:

- As the boat flips over, if you are quick you can end up sitting on the uppermost side of the boat
- You can then swiftly step over the boat and stand on the centreboard
- Using your weight, lean on the centreboard to pull the boat back upright
- As the boat rights itself, step back over the side into the cockpit, keeping yourself dry

As before, you can then sort out all the ropes, making sure nothing is tangled, open any drainage points and start sailing again.

If you are quick, you can step over onto the centreboard

Simply apply all your weight to the centreboard and step back aboard as the boat comes up

TWO-PERSON DINGHY

Two-person boats tend to be larger than one-person boats and, as such, are slightly harder to pull back upright.

Good communication is vital during the procedure as the two people will eventually end up on opposite sides of the boat and out of sight of each other. Knowing what the other is doing is important to avoid confusion or being unprepared.

The method we will illustrate is called the scoop method, where one person pulls the boat up whilst the other person is scooped back aboard.

When the boat capsizes, both helm and crew end up in the water. The first step is to check that they are both okay and not caught up in any loose ropes.

Next, they check that the centreboard is extended fully as this will be needed later.

They need to decide who is going to take the lead role and swim around to the centreboard. This should be the heavier person. In our example this is the helmsman who swims to the stern of the boat, taking the mainsheet with him. When at the stern, he double checks that the rudder hasn't fallen off. Meanwhile, the crew stays where he is but must be prepared to swim free should he feel the boat begin to invert.

The helmsman then swims to the centreboard, still holding on to the mainsheet.

At the same time, on the other side of the boat, the crew is positioning himself in the water. He should grab hold of something secure in the cockpit, which will allow him to be scooped aboard. It is important that he doesn't apply too much pressure and fight against the efforts of the helmsman, who is working on the opposite side to right the boat.

The crew should try to free the mainsheet fully as this will stop the sail from powering up as soon as the boat is upright again.

The helmsman then pushes down on the centreboard, applying a constant pressure. However, he may need to give the centreboard a sharp pump with his body weight to break the surface tension caused by the sail sticking to the water. The boat will then right itself quickly.

With the boat now upright, the crew is able to help the helmsman climb aboard. In our illustrations this is over the stern of the boat as the transom is low. If you choose this option, be prepared to move quickly because your weight will act as a sea anchor and make the boat turn away from the wind, increasing the chance of yet another capsize. Do not climb in under the boom as the extra weight will pull the boat back over.

Once aboard, the helmsman and crew sort out all the ropes, making sure nothing is tangled, and open any drainage points before sailing off again.

The helmsman and crew are in the water. Check you are free from all loose ropes

The helmsman checks the rudder is in place

And swims to the centreboard, still holding the mainsheet

Meanwhile the crew ensures the mainsheet is fully slack

And floats in the water, holding the boat

The helmsman applies a spurt of pressure to the centreboard to pull the mainsail out of the water

And continues to apply steady gentle pressure to the centreboard

As the boat comes up, the crew is scooped aboard

The crew then helps the helmsman aboard

DEALING WITH AN INVERSION

An inverted capsize is when the boat turns 180° and ends up fully upside down, with the mast in the water and the centreboard pointing upwards.

This is a common occurrence as, due to the built-in buoyancy design of most dinghies, when the boat capsizes, the hull can be lifted high in the water with the mast pointing in a downward angle. Gravity then simply pulls the boat to the inverted position.

When this happens do not worry. A bit more effort is required but done correctly should not be too much of a strain. Both helm and crew swim to the windward side of the boat, climb out of the water and stand on the upturned gunwale, grabbing hold of the centreboard. They need to be careful with the trailing edge of the centreboard as this is thin and delicate and can be very easily damaged.

The helm and crew just lean back, pulling in the same direction. There's no need to apply too much force here as a gentle and sustained pressure will suffice and is the key to an effective capsize procedure.

Slowly the boat will adopt the flat capsize position, whereby it is lying on its side.

The lighter person should then swim back around the rear of the boat and end up on the cockpit side, taking care to stay in direct contact with the boat. Both helm and crew then follow the process described previously.

When inverted, both helmsman and crew stand on the gunwale, hold the centreboard and then lean back

They apply consistent pressure to force the boat to move

And keep pushing on the centreboard until the boat is flat

The lighter person swims to the cockpit side and prepares to be scooped aboard as before

CAPSIZE PRACTICE

A well-practised capsize drill is an important skill to master and is preferable to leaving it until you have to, which is likely to be on a windy day when things happen beyond your control. Practise in light winds so you know what to do when the need arises.

First choose a safe area that is deep enough to take the mast should you fully invert. To force the boat to capsize, lean on the boom and push this towards the water. If sailing a two-person boat, both of you should do this as the imbalance of weight will knock the boat over. When in the water, go through the routine already described above.

Push on the boom to force a capsize

Keep pushing until the boat falls over

OTHER SAFETY MATTERS
RIGHTING LINES

Some boats are fitted with righting lines. These are lines connected to the hull on both sides. They serve no useful purpose during general sailing, but in the event of a capsize can make things easier. It is purely down to personal choice as to whether you fit these lines or not. By using them, you may be able to apply more turning pressure to the upturned or capsized hull.

KEEP A LOOKOUT

It is vital to keep a good lookout at all times when sailing. In particular, pay attention under the sails as boats can come at you from any angle.

Bear in mind that the wind will often make it hard to hear approaching vessels, especially another sailing boat, so a good lookout is essential. It is the responsibility of everyone afloat to avoid collisions, regardless of who is 'in the right', so be prepared to take avoiding action or stop to prevent a collision.

For more information on rules please read the Rules of the Road chapter on page 177.

Always keep a good lookout and avoid collisions

RESCUE
ATTRACTING ATTENTION

As mentioned, the best place to sail is somewhere there is a safety boat in operation. If you need to catch the safety boat's attention, stop the boat and allow the sails to flap. Stand up if you are able to do so and make large arm movements to further attract the attention of the safety boat crew.

Make big arm movements to attract attention

You may even consider lowering the mainsail if your boat is fitted with a halyard or release the clew outhaul on the mainsail to let the sail flap. This will draw more attention to yourself.

UNDER TOW

If you need to be towed ashore, the safety boat crew will instruct you on what to do but, with the sails lowered, the crew should take the tow rope from the safety boat and wrap it completely around the mast, holding it tight. Do not tie this off – you may need to release it quickly, so having the rope looped around the mast allows you to do so.

Wrap tow rope around the mast and hold tight. DO NOT tie the rope fast

You may need to let the tow boat slip in a hurry

Either raise the centreboard before being towed ...

... or remove the daggerboard

Single person holds tow rope and steers

The safety crew will then secure the tow rope to their boat and slowly take up the slack. You then steer to follow the safety boat. Near the shore, or when instructed to do so, simply let go of the tow rope and use your paddle for the last little bit.

MAN OVERBOARD (MOB)

If you fall overboard in a single-person boat, the boat will usually either capsize or gently turn towards the wind and stop. Simply swim towards the boat and climb aboard. However, the force of the wind on the unmanned boat may be stronger than your ability to swim. This is one of the reasons why you should never sail alone. If you remain in the water the safety boat should spot you and come to pick you out of the water.

If the boat has capsized, follow the procedure for a capsize earlier in this chapter.

In a two-person boat, if one person falls overboard the remaining person should immediately check the position of the casualty in the water and keep the person in view, taking control of the tiller.

Bear in mind that it is easy to become disorientated, particularly in this situation, so try to link the casualty in the water to a fixed landmark.

First turn onto a beam reach on your current tack, which is when the wind is blowing across the boat. Sail away for about 25 metres. This distance is important as it will allow you to adopt a more controlled approach to the casualty.

Turn the boat around by tacking slowly through the wind (see the How to Tack chapter on page 113) and turn onto the broad reach on the other tack. Try to keep sight of the casualty at all times.

Sail past the casualty slowly by letting the jib flap and control the mainsail so it mostly flaps to ensure you approach slowly. (Use your masthead burgee or flags ashore to judge where the wind is blowing from).

The last thing you want to do is run the casualty over at speed!

Continue sailing until you are slightly downwind of the casualty.

When you are approximately three metres away from the casualty, turn the boat back towards the wind so you approach on a close reach point of sailing. This will take you slowly towards the casualty. Leave the mainsheet so the sail flaps but be prepared to pull it in slightly if you go too slowly.

Steer to approach the casualty so he is on the windward side of the boat, opposite the boom. This will make it easier to deal with the casualty and reduce the chance of him pulling the boat over when he climbs back aboard.

Help the casualty aboard by pulling on his buoyancy aid. This can either be near the shrouds or, if your boat has an open transom, it may be easier to pull him in over the stern.

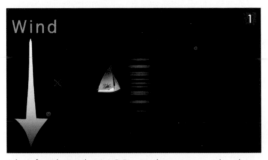

Identify where the MOB is in the water and sail away on a beam reach

After 25 metres tack round, keeping sight of the MOB

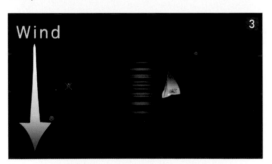

Start to drop below the MOB by sailing on a broad reach

When below the MOB start to turn towards the wind to slow down

Travelling slowly, approach the MOB so he is opposite the boom

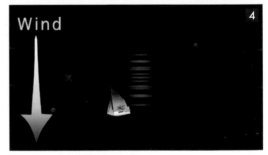

Recover the MOB back on board

It is a good idea to practise this man overboard manoeuvre using a suitable floating object weighted down with some rope to give ballast. The secret is controlling your final approach speed and aim to stop right by the casualty.

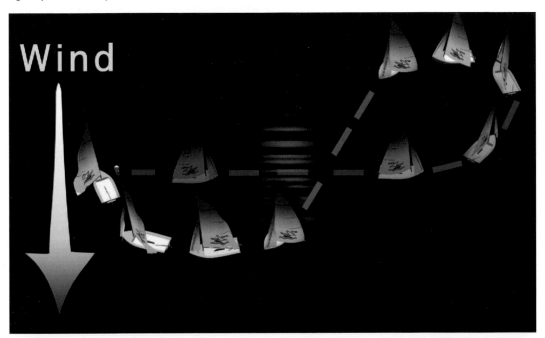

Man overboard path

KEY LEARNING POINTS

- Dinghies do not sink when they capsize.
- Everyone capsizes, even the most experienced sailors, so don't be worried or embarrassed.
- Swim to the stern and make sure the rudder is in place.
- Ensure the centreboard is pushed fully down.
- Hold the mainsheet to keep in direct contact with the boat at all times, preventing you from being separated.
- Remember to apply consistent, gentle pressure to the centreboard or righting lines to pull the boat back up.
- Release the mainsheet fully so when the boat comes upright the sail will automatically flap.
- When the boat is flat on its side it may be necessary to give the centreboard a sharp pump to break the surface tension caused by the sail sticking to the water.
- In a two-person boat, the lighter person should position themselves by the cockpit in preparation to be scooped up, but he should be careful not to apply any force that will counterbalance the helmsman who is trying to right the boat from the centreboard.
- Once the lighter person has been scooped up, he should help the other person to get back aboard.
- Communication throughout the procedure of righting a boat is essential to ensure it is smooth and safe.
- A good capsize drill is an important part of sailing. Being completely familiar with what you need to do allows you to be more confident with your general sailing.

ASYMMETRIC SPINNAKER

A SPINNAKER IS A LIGHTWEIGHT SAIL THAT CAN DRAMATICALLY INCREASE YOUR SPEED & FUN AFLOAT

Go online for a video demonstration: www.fernhurstbooks.com – search for *Sailing: A Beginner's Guide* and click on 'Additional resources'.

The spinnaker is a large sail made of lightweight sail cloth and is used on a downwind point of sailing. Generally only used on two-person boats, it will add a whole new dimension of fun to your sailing. In this chapter you will learn how to rig and use an asymmetric spinnaker.

The asymmetric spinnaker is flown from a bowsprit which on many boats extends and retracts automatically when the sail is hoisted and lowered.

Asymmetric spinnakers have now all but superseded conventional symmetric spinnakers in modern boat design and are widely used on dinghies, keel boats and modern yachts.

The spinnaker can only be used when the boat is on a beam reach, broad reach or training run. It cannot be used on a close-hauled or close reach point of sailing.

Contrary to the information on centreboard position given in the Points of Sailing chapter on page 37, when sailing with an asymmetric spinnaker it is normal to leave the centreboard fully down at all times. The reason for this is that the increase of speed that the sail will introduce will push what is called the apparent wind more towards the bow.

Apparent wind is the combination of true wind direction and forward speed of the boat. Although you are actually sailing in a direction away from or across the wind, the apparent wind will trick the boat into behaving as though it were on a close reach or even close-hauled point of sailing, where the centreboard should be fully lowered.

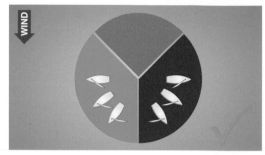

A spinnaker can only be used when the boat is on a beam reach, broad reach or training run

A spinnaker cannot be used on close-hauled or close reach points of sailing

The asymmetric spinnaker is flown from a bowsprit

RIGGING THE SAIL

It is your choice as to whether you rig the spinnaker before or after the jib, but to make it clearer in the pictures we have opted to rig the spinnaker first.

Like the other sails, the spinnaker has three corners called the head, the tack and the clew and it is hoisted using the spinnaker halyard.

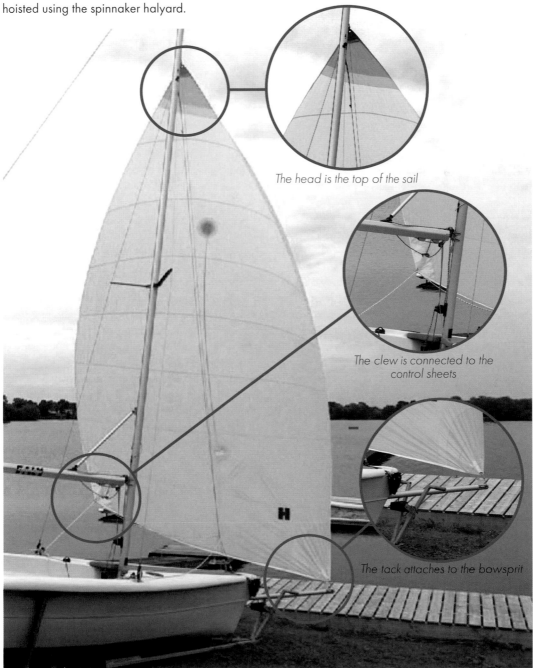

The head is the top of the sail

The clew is connected to the control sheets

The tack attaches to the bowsprit

The spinnaker has 3 corners

TOP TIP

The spinnaker is easy to rig upside down. To ensure you rig the sail the right way up, use a permanent pen to write HEAD on the top corner of the sail and TACK on the lower corner of the sail that connects to the bowsprit.

Firstly, pick up the end of the spinnaker halyard and pull it off to one side of the boat. Look up to make sure it is not tangled around the other rigging.

Next, attach the head of the sail to the end of the halyard using a bowline knot. The bowline is the best knot to use as it works well under load and can be untied easily afterwards. To learn how to tie a bowline, see page 167.

You then run your hands along the leading edge, or luff, of the sail until you find the next corner of the sail, called the tack, which is usually marked.

Tie this corner of the sail to the bowsprit, again preferably using a bowline knot.

The sail is lowered with a retrieval line. This is in fact the tail end of the spinnaker halyard and it emerges from the spinnaker chute. Pass the end of this line through the lower and first of two retrieval patches on the sail. These are strengthened circular patches. Pull more of the retrieval line through and finally tie it to the second patch on the spinnaker, again using a bowline knot.

Next, you should fully hoist the sail to check nothing is tangled. Position the boat so the bow is pointing away from the wind, and hoist the sail, being careful to make sure that it doesn't get caught on the trolley.

TOP TIP

When attaching the retrieval line, it is a good idea to part raise the spinnaker. This will make it easier to tie the line to the sail.

If it is windy, beware that the wind could catch the sail and blow the boat off the trolley, causing some damage.

When the sail is hoisted, the next step is to rig the remaining control sheets. Pass one of these sheets around the front of the forestay and thread it through the control fairlead on the deck, which should be near the wire shrouds at the side of the boat.

Tie a figure-of-eight knot in the end of the sheet (see page 164) to prevent it running free. Next, rig the remaining sheet in the same way and tie both ends of the spinnaker sheets together as this makes things easier when sailing.

With the ropes all connected correctly you should then pull the sail into the spinnaker chute. Release the halyard and pull on the retrieval line. It is important to keep the halyard under slight tension to stop the sail from falling on the ground or getting caught on the trolley.

You then rig the jib, as described on page 26. Once the jib is rigged, you may choose to move the forestay out of the way by tying this back to the mast. The forestay is the wire rigging that stops the mast from falling backwards when the sails are lowered. With the jib rigged, the forestay is redundant. By moving the forestay, you alleviate the risk of the sail snagging and tearing on the bare wire, and the furling action of the jib is also made easier if the forestay is out of the way.

Simply untie the forestay from the bow of the boat and secure it at the mast to stop it flying free. However, if you do this you MUST remember to reconnect the forestay before you lower the jib at the end of your sailing session, otherwise the mast will fall down!

Rig the jib and remove the forestay

Attach the head to the halyard with a bowline knot

Run your hands along the edge of the sail to make sure it is not tangled

Locate the tack of the sail

Attach the tack to the bowsprit with a bowline knot

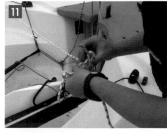

Pass the retrieval line through the first downhaul patch of the sail

Locate the second downhaul patch

Tie the end of the retrieval line to the second patch using a bowline knot

With the control sheets attached to the clew, hoist the sail ashore to check for tangles)

Pass one control line around the forestay (or jib if rigged)

Pass the control sheet through the fairlead on the deck

Repeat on the other side and tie both control sheets together with a reef knot

Pull on the retrieval line to retract the sail into the chute

HOW TO LAUNCH THE SAIL

Once afloat, the first point to understand is when you can actually hoist the sail. As mentioned, this is best done on a training run. Remember that you cannot launch the sail when on a close-hauled or even close reach point of sailing. The sail simply flaps like a flag and will not work.

Teamwork is crucial. Working together, the helmsman and crew balance the boat to keep it flat. The crew then pulls the spinnaker up using the halyard.

This may feel tight because pulling the sail up also extends the bowsprit. Watch out here as

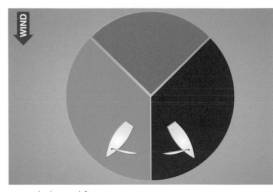

Launch the sail from a training run

the sail will suddenly pull free from the spinnaker chute, so make sure the crew is well balanced or even seated to do this. The crew then locks the spinnaker halyard in the jam cleat, which is usually located on the floor of the boat near the foot of the mast.

The crew pulls the halyard to hoist the sail

The sail pops free from the chute

The crew picks up the control sheet

The sail emerges from the chute and the bowsprit extends automatically

The crew locks the halyard in the cleat

Check the sail is fully hoisted

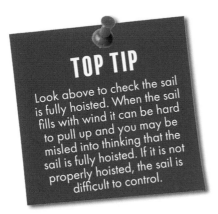

TOP TIP

Look above to check the sail is fully hoisted. When the sail fills with wind it can be hard to pull up and you may be misled into thinking that the sail is fully hoisted. If it is not properly hoisted, the sail is difficult to control.

The crew tightens the spinnaker sheet to retain the sail shape

TRIMMING THE SAIL

With the sail fully hoisted, the crew moves to pick up the leeward control sheet. This is the one on the same side as the boom. The spinnaker sheet is the control line that is used to set the sail in the optimum position. To find this point the crew releases the sheet a few inches at a time until the luff just starts to flicker. When this happens, the crew then pulls the sheet back to the point where the sail stops flapping.

If the sheet is eased too much, the whole sail will start to flap.

If the sheet is released too far, the whole sail will flap

The crew eases the sheet until the luff of the sail flickers

The crew adjusts the spinnaker sheet constantly and when the luff flutters, he pulls the sheet in once more.

Boat approaching gybe

TOP TIP

Always wear gloves when using the spinnaker. If not there is a high risk of friction burns from the pressure of the rope either sliding through your hands or simply by holding tight.

Helm checks gybe area is clear

HOW TO GYBE WITH A SPINNAKER

Sooner or later you are going to have to gybe, and in this chapter we are assuming that you have read and understood the chapter on How to Gybe (see page 123).

During the gybe, the actions undertaken by the helm are pretty much the same. The crew, however, has more to do. To start with, practise your gybing in light winds when things happen slowly:

- Establish the boat on a broad reach or training run
- The helmsman checks the area is clear and shouts 'standby to gybe'
- The crew in turn double checks the area and picks up the new spinnaker sheet, releasing the jibsheet and replying 'all clear'
- The helmsman then initiates the turn and controls the point when the boom flicks across by pulling on the mainsheet falls when the weight of the mainsheet feels light
- As the boom moves over, both of you must DUCK and get ready to move your weight quickly to the other side to balance the boat
- The crew starts to pull the spinnaker across onto the new side with the new spinnaker sheet
- As soon as the spinnaker is fully out on the other side, the crew looks at the luff of the sail and adjusts the sheet to find the point where the luff starts to curl
- Finally the crew pulls in and cleats the jibsheet to stop the jib from flapping

Helm initiates the gybe as the crew pulls the spinnaker across

Crew pulls the spinnaker across and both move to balance the boat

Boat bears away

Helm and crew prepare to gybe

Helm positioned in the centre of the boat ready to start the turn

Crew picks up new spinnaker sheet and helm pulls the mainsheet falls

The boom moves across; helm and crew balance the boat

Boom flicks across the boat

Crew adjusts the jib on the new side and maintains attention on the spinnaker

Boat sails on the new gybe

LOWERING THE SAIL

When you are ready to lower the sail, turn the boat back onto a training run. This will put most of the spinnaker behind the mainsail, which will dramatically reduce the force of the wind in the sail.

The crew passes the spinnaker sheet to the helm so that he can keep the sail under control. The crew then releases the spinnaker halyard and pulls on the retrieval line to retrieve the sail. It is important to maintain slight tension in the halyard to prevent the sail from falling in the water and the boat running over it. On most boat designs nowadays, the bowsprit is automatically retracted when the sail is lowered.

Before dropping the spinnaker, turn the boat onto a training run; the crew passes the helm the spinnaker sheet

The crew prepares to lower the spinnaker

And releases the halyard

The crew pulls on the retrieval line

The spinnaker and bowsprit retract simultaneously

156

WHAT TO DO WHEN IT'S WINDY

When the wind increases, it is highly likely that the boat will plane. This happens when a gust of wind hits the boat and the increase in power lifts the bow clear of the water. The boat skims along the surface with just the rear most section of the hull in contact with the water.

Boat starting to plane

The bow lifts clear of the water and the speed increases

Lean or move backwards slightly to promote planing

Travelling at speed calls for careful concentration and good teamwork. Good balance is also critical. You must keep the boat flat and be prepared to move your weight extremely quickly around the boat as required.

DEALING WITH GUSTS OF WIND

A good skill to develop is how to spot a gust of wind and what to do when it hits the boat. It is better to be prepared for this rather than feel the panic that sets in if you get caught out.

Gusts appear as darker patches on the surface of the water. When you see one approaching, be prepared to bear away from the wind just a little.

At the same time the crew eases the spinnaker sheet slightly, looking for the point where the luff just starts to flicker.

Continue in this direction until you feel the gust passing. Once it has passed you and the boat starts to slow, luff up slightly to increase the airflow across the spinnaker again.

When a gust hits, bear away slightly

Continue on the same course until the gust passes

When the gust passes, luff up again

Repeat this process as and when further gusts hit you. This combination of bearing away from the wind when the gust hits and luffing up when it has passed is the best practice. Done successfully, you should avoid capsizing and get the best out of the wind.

GYBING ON A WINDY DAY

In time, speed will become your friend and you will learn to gybe when travelling fast as the load on the rig is reduced due to the boat's forward motion. However, to begin with gybing can be extremely daunting because it all happens incredibly quickly. So until you are confident, it is a good idea to let any gusts of wind pass you by before attempting to gybe.

The techniques used by the helm and crew are the same as previously described on page 154, but in windy conditions the boom will fly across the boat very speedily indeed.

The normal gybe routine applies in the wind

But things happen much faster

Be prepared to balance the boat extremely quickly

CAPSIZING WITH A SPINNAKER

It is a certainty that you will capsize at some point with your spinnaker up. No matter how experienced you become, the extra power of the sail will lead to inevitable capsizes.

In this chapter we assume you have already read the Capsize & Recovery chapter on page 133. The only difference here is what you do with the extra sail.

As with a normal capsize, the heavier person will swim around to the centreboard, leaving the lighter person inside the cockpit. If the crew is the lighter person, then he releases the spinnaker halyard and simply pulls the sail back inside its launching chute with the retrieval line.

This makes things much easier when pulling the boat back up and reduces the chance of capsizing the boat for a second time.

Once the sail is safely lowered and put away, the conventional capsize procedure then applies (see page 138).

A capsize is common with the spinnaker

The spinnaker should be lowered before the boat is pulled upright

The heavier person should be on the centreboard with the lighter person lowering the sail

When the sail is lowered and stowed away, the normal recovery procedure applies

COMMON MISTAKES

Most of the mistakes when dealing with a spinnaker will probably result in the boat capsizing!

- Not rigging the sail correctly will lead to the sail becoming tangled when hoisted or rigged upside down.
- Not hoisting the sail from a training run. This could result in the sail filling with wind before you are ready and causing the boat to capsize.
- Not bearing away from the wind when a gust hits could capsize you.
- Not moving your weight across to balance the boat during a gybe will lead to capsizing.
- Not keeping the halyard slightly tensioned when lowering the sail will result in the sail being run over by the boat.

Spinnaker rigged upside down

KEY LEARNING POINTS

- The spinnaker is a large sail that can only be used when the boat is on a beam reach, broad reach or training run.
- The spinnaker cannot be used on a close-hauled or close reach point of sailing.
- Leave the centreboard fully down.
- When rigging, ensure all the control sheets are outside any other rigging lines, including the retrieval line.
- Use a bowline knot to secure the halyard.
- Run your hands along the leading edge of the sail when rigging to make sure it is not tangled.
- Tie the ends of the sheets together to allow better control when gybing.
- If your forestay is removable, it is advisable to relocate this to the mast to prevent the wire snagging the sail. Remember though to reconnect the forestay before lowering the jib at the end of your sail.
- The sail is launched from a chute at the bow of the boat and is hoisted with its own halyard.
- Hoist the sail on a training run point of sailing, and then adjust your point of sailing to get where you want to go.
- The crew is responsible for managing the spinnaker and he should release and tighten the spinnaker control sheets to find the point where the edge of the sail starts to curl. This is the most efficient setting for the sail.
- Turn the boat away from the wind when a gust hits and then turn back when it has passed.
- During the gybe, the crew pulls the spinnaker across.
- To drop the spinnaker, turn the boat back onto a training run.

KNOTS

KNOTS ARE IMPORTANT TO LEARN AS THEY WILL ALLOW YOU TO UNTIE A PIECE OF ROPE EASILY. THIS CHAPTER FOCUSES ON THE MOST COMMON TYPES FOR DINGHY SAILING

Go online for a video demonstration: www.fernhurstbooks.com – search for *Sailing: A Beginner's Guide* and click on 'Additional resources'.

Knowing how to tie knots correctly is important, not only because you want to be sure that whatever you have secured will stay that way, but also because you will want to be able to untie a knot, even after a very heavy load has been applied. The wind can put tremendous force on any control line, so you must be sure that whatever item is secured is done so with a suitable knot.

You should practise the knots we show you below and be able to tie them blindfolded. Only then will you be familiar enough with each knot to be able to tie them quickly.

There are dozens of knots in existence. Most have specific uses, and a few are purely decorative. Entire publications are dedicated to the subject, but we will just illustrate the most common and useful knots for dinghy sailing.

FIGURE-OF-EIGHT

This is a frequently used knot and one of the easiest to tie. It is sometimes called a stopper knot because it can be used to prevent a rope from pulling free from a fairlead or jam cleat. It is used at the end of control lines

Start with the rope in one hand

Bend the tail and pass it back across the standing part of the rope

Bend the tail back around and under the standing part

Position the tail so you can poke it through the loop from above

Finally, grab both tails and pull tight

The finished knot

REEF KNOT

Sometimes known as the square knot, this is a general purpose knot used to join two pieces of rope together. Not to be confused with a granny knot, the reef knot remains easy to undo.

Start by holding both pieces of rope you want to tie together in separate hands. Pass the left-hand piece of rope over the top of the right-hand piece

Bend this around and back under, pulling a bit of slack through

Bend both tails back towards each other so they point together

Next pass the tail of rope in your right hand over the left-hand piece and back under. Then pull both tails tight

The finished knot

ROUND TURN & TWO HALF HITCHES

This is a great knot that is used to tie a single piece of rope to a fixed object. It is particularly useful when tying a boat to a cleat on a pontoon or to its trolley, as the main loop of the knot bears all the load, and the half hitches secure the knot in place. This knot works well under load but remains easy to untie when required.

Take the tail of the rope and pass it around the fixed object twice

Bend the tail over the standing part and thread the tail through the gap that appears between the tail and the fixed object

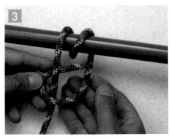

Pull the tail tight. This creates the first 'hitch'

Repeat the process to make the second hitch

Bend the tail back upwards, poking the tail through the hole that appears below the first hitch

Pull tight

CLOVE HITCH

This is an alternative to the round turn and two half hitches.

Pass the tail of the rope over the top of the fixed object and bring the tail back towards you

Cross the tail over the top of the standing part of the rope

Bend the tail over the top of the fixed object and back towards you and poke the tail back up through the gap that has appeared

Pull tight

BOWLINE

This is perhaps the most complex of the simple knots to master, but it is worth persevering as it is probably the most useful knot to a sailor.

The bowline is used to create a fixed single loop in the end of a line.

It is very strong under load and can be used for many purposes on the boat, such as tying a sheet to the clew of a sail or securing the painter to a ring or post.

It is also very easy to untie.

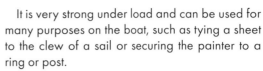

Start by holding the tail of the piece of rope in both hands

Make a small loop in the standing part of the rope so the top of the loop is on top of the standing part of the rope

Pick up the tail and pass this up through the loop from underneath

Thread the tail underneath the standing part of the rope

Take the tail and pass behind the standing part of the rope

Finally, bend the tail back around the standing part and thread it down through the loop from the top

Tail is poked though the loop

Pull tight

REEFING

REEFING IS THE PROCEDURE THAT ALLOWS YOU TO REDUCE THE AMOUNT OF SAIL AREA. THE SMALLER SAIL IS EASIER TO HANDLE IN STRONGER WINDS

Go online for a video demonstration: www.fernhurstbooks.com – search for *Sailing: A Beginner's Guide* and click on 'Additional resources'.

Reefing is the process that allows you to reduce the amount of sail area by either folding or rolling the sail. Having a smaller sail will enable you to control the boat without being overpowered in stronger winds. While you are learning how to sail, it is better to do things slowly under control rather than fight with an overpowered boat.

With a reefed sail, you will be able to focus on your sailing skills yet still be able to experience the pleasure of sailing in strong winds. You will probably find that you will end up sailing faster, capsize less and have a more enjoyable time with a reefed sail rather than with a full-sized sail.

Each reef takes out approximately 20 percent of the sail area. The more you take out, the more controllable the boat becomes in a strong wind. You should judge for yourself as to whether you need to apply a second or even third reef. If you need to make additional reefs, just repeat the process described below.

Reefing is best done ashore before you leave the beach or pontoon and, if in doubt, put a reef in before you go out.

REEFING AN UNSTAYED SINGLE-PERSON BOAT

Let's look first at reefing a single-person boat with an unstayed mast.

These types of boat do not have any wire supporting rigging to hold the mast up and the sail simply wraps around the mast in the reefing process.

With the boat head to wind, the first step is to release the clew outhaul from the end of the boom. It is important to keep hold of the sail because if you don't, there is a risk the flapping sail could hit you in the face.

Once you have the clew, walk towards the bow of the boat taking the sail with you.

When you get to the mast, simply wrap the whole sail around the mast for one complete revolution. Each turn reduces the sail area by approximately 20 percent, so keep reducing the sail area until you are comfortable with the size of sail.

Take the clew of the sail back towards the end of the boom in preparation for reconnecting it to the boom.

Unclip the clew from the boom

Grab hold of the sail, being careful the flapping sail does not hit you, and wrap the sail around the mast the required number of times

Reconnect the clew, tie down and outhaul

Release the clew tie down

Pick up the clew of the mainsail

Pull the clew outhaul tight

Release and extend the outhaul line and reconnect this to the clew of the sail. Note that you may need to fit a short extension if the outhaul is not long enough.

Reconnect the clew, tie down and finally pull the clew outhaul back tight.

A single-person sail after reefing

TOP TIP

With the sail reefed, the outhaul rope from the end of the boom to the clew of the sail will be long. This will mean that the sail will ride up above the boom when sailing and will be difficult to control. To prevent this, ensure that the clew is tied to the boom with a strap or rope.

REEFING A TWO-PERSON BOAT

Two-person boats usually have wire rigging to support the mast. This will prevent you from wrapping the sail around the mast to reef.

The process for reefing a two-person boat is called slab reefing, where 'slabs' of the mainsail are folded from the bottom or foot of the sail.

Cruising sails will have two or sometimes three reefing points to allow different amounts of sail to be taken out. Each reef will take away approximately 20 percent of the sail area.

The reefing line is the main control line for the reefing process. This line has two ends, one at the mast end of the boom and the second at the outer edge of the boom. A pulley system threaded inside the boom allows the line to be pulled tight from a third point, as shown in steps 12 and 13.

The first step is to park the boat head to wind and rig the full sail. The reason for this is that the foot of the sail can easily become disconnected during the reefing process and flap around above your head when sailing. Rigging the full sail with both the tack and clew ends of the mainsail secured will help prevent this.

- Release the reefing line from its jam cleat on the boom and pull all the slack through.
- To make the process simpler, you can release the main halyard and part lower the sail. This will make it easier to reach the reefing points on the sail.
- Then thread the mast end of the reefing line through to the desired reefing point.
- Pass the line between the sail and the kicking strap (if your boat has a kicking strap that pushes the boom down – see page 17). Note that if you go outside the kicking strap, the reef will not be completed

Most mainsails have more than one reefing point

properly.
- Take the line back to the boom and secure it with a bowline knot around the gooseneck.
- Next, go to the clew end of the boom and pull the slack out of the reefing line.
- Thread the reefing line though the holes in the back edge or leech of the sail until you come to your desired reefing point. (Note that there could be several holes before the reinforced clew reefing point is reached.)
- Thread the line through this new clew and return the line to the boom.

Most boats have a loose fitted mainsail, so it is best to tie the reefing line to the boom using a bowline knot around the boom. The reason for this is that when the reefing line is tensioned, the clew of the sail is held tightly to the boom. This makes the sail easier to control.

- Return to the mast end of the boom and start to pull the reefing line tight.
- You may need to release the main halyard in small amounts; continue at the same time to pull the reefing line until the desired reefing point is just above the boom.
- When this point is reached, pull the main halyard tight again to make sure the sail is in the correct position.
- To finish off, you will need to tidy up the reefing line to stop it getting tangled.
- The sail may be fitted with reefing ties and these should be tied with a reef knot.
- If it is particularly windy, you may need to repeat this process with the second reef in the mainsail.

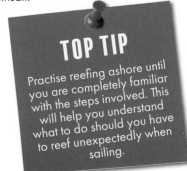

TOP TIP

Practise reefing ashore until you are completely familiar with the steps involved. This will help you understand what to do should you have to reef unexpectedly when sailing.

Start with a fully rigged sail

Release the reefing line from the mast end of the boom

Release the main halyard

Part lower the mainsail

Pull the slack through and thread the reefing line through the reefing point on the sail

Pass the reefing line through the sail and go UNDER the kicking strap

Tie the reefing line back to the boom with a bowline knot

Go to the clew end of the boom and pull the reefing line out

Thread the reefing line through the holes in the sail

Continue threading until the desired reefing point is reached

Tie the reefing line back to the boom with a bowline around the boom

Pull the reefing line

Continue to pull until the reefing point is in line with the boom

Gather up the surplus folds of the sail

Tidy up the loose folds and secure with reefing ties

Reefed mainsail

PRACTISE YOUR TECHNIQUE

As mentioned, it is best to reef in advance of going afloat, but you should practise reefing afloat in controlled conditions. This will help you to identify what to do for real should the need arise.

For example, you may go day sailing on a nice sunny day when the wind is light in the morning. In coastal waters, it is common on summer afternoons for a sea breeze to fill in. This is the effect of the sun warming the land, causing hot air to rise, with colder air rushing in from the sea to take its place.

The sea breeze can increase the wind dramatically, which may mean you need to reef whilst afloat, so having practised in light winds you should know what to do.

Reefing when afloat is best done from the hove-to position (see page 110) on a close reach point of sailing. Ask the crew to pull the jib across onto the wrong side whilst you steer a steady course.

When in the hove-to position, the boom will flutter out of the way to one side of the boat. The crew then carries out the reefing procedure as described above.

Practise reefing afloat by adopting the hove-to position

Helmsman steers and steadies the boat while the crew reefs the sail

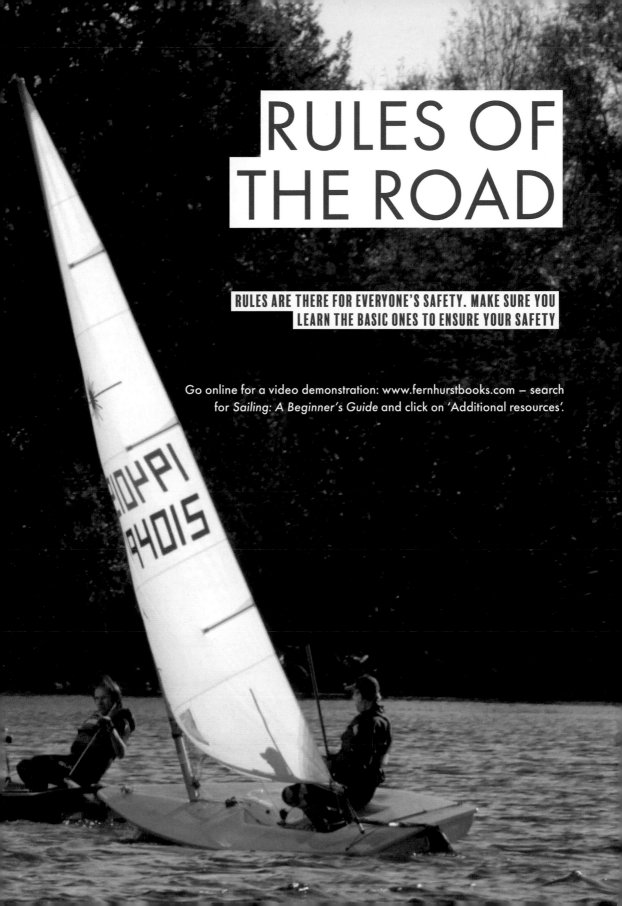

RULES OF THE ROAD

RULES ARE THERE FOR EVERYONE'S SAFETY. MAKE SURE YOU LEARN THE BASIC ONES TO ENSURE YOUR SAFETY

Go online for a video demonstration: www.fernhurstbooks.com – search for *Sailing: A Beginner's Guide* and click on 'Additional resources'.

Rules are there for everyone's safety. They are in place to make it clear to everyone on the water who has priority for any particular situation. The basic rules we will be illustrating form only a small part of *The International Regulations for Preventing Collisions* at Sea or *IRPCS*. This is a weighty publication laying out the regulations for all vessels afloat, including heavy commercial shipping.

Understanding the rules allows people to sail in close proximity with other boats

This chapter focuses on the fundamental rules and covers the most common situations. As a dinghy sailor you must at least have knowledge of these, but also be aware that other regulations do apply in certain situations, mainly when racing. If you plan to race, you should research these additional rules separately – entire books have been written on this subject and as such are beyond the scope of this chapter.

AVOID A COLLISION

When afloat, the priority of all vessels is to avoid a collision or any incident. The most basic rule that you must observe always is to keep a good lookout at all times. Be prepared to take avoiding action in plenty of time, even if you think you should not be the one to give way; the oncoming vessel simply may not have seen you.

Keep a good lookout at all times for approaching vessels

Do not forget to look under the boom as well as behind your back as boats can come at you from any angle. Be aware that the wind may restrict your ability to hear the sounds of approaching vessels and sailing boats in particular can be hard to hear.

Further racing rules apply which are beyond the scope of this chapter

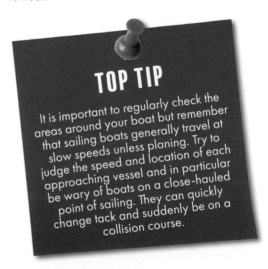

TOP TIP

It is important to regularly check the areas around your boat but remember that sailing boats generally travel at slow speeds unless planing. Try to judge the speed and location of each approaching vessel and in particular be wary of boats on a close-hauled point of sailing. They can quickly change tack and suddenly be on a collision course.

WHO HAS PRIORITY?

Vessels are described as being the 'give way' vessel and the 'stand on' vessel. Note that no boats are described as being the 'right of way' vessel. Regardless of the situation, it is everyone's priority to avoid a collision afloat, but the 'give way' vessel is the vessel that should take the avoiding action first.

When taking avoiding action, it is best to steer behind the oncoming vessel rather than chance your luck and dash in front.

Always be prepared to take avoiding action

SAIL VERSUS POWER

In most situations sail has priority over powerboats, which should keep out of your way. However, you must keep clear of large commercial shipping or fishing vessels; they are often constrained by their draught or their manoeuvrability.

You must also keep out of the way of any man-powered vessels like rowing boats.

TOP TIP

Motor vessels can travel significantly faster than a sailing dinghy and, even if they seem a long way away, can reach you much sooner than you think, so keep a constant lookout at all times. Bear in mind that at sea level, the horizon is only about three miles away so fast boats can cover that distance very quickly.

Power gives way to sail, but keep clear of commercial and fishing shipping

POINTS OF SAILING

This topic is covered in detail in the Points of Sailing chapter on page 37, but any point of sailing where the wind is on the left-hand side of the boat is called port tack and is the 'give way' tack.

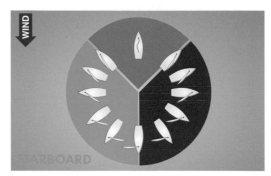

Boats with the wind on their right-hand side are on starboard tack

Boats with the wind on their left-hand side are on port tack

Any point of sailing where the wind is on the right-hand side of the boat is called starboard tack, which is the 'stand on' tack.

You must familiarise yourself with what point of sailing and what tack you are on at all times, as this has a direct bearing on whether you are the 'give way' vessel or not.

If you are the boat on starboard, it is more likely that you are the 'stand on' vessel, in which case you can alert your position to oncoming traffic on port tack by shouting loudly 'starboard'. But you must be prepared to take avoiding action if the boat on port does not respond.

Boats on starboard can shout 'starboard' to alert the attention of oncoming port tack boats

PORT VERSUS STARBOARD

This can come in a variety of guises. Fundamentally, the boat on port is the 'give way' vessel and should keep clear of the boat on starboard. That said, the boat on port often has choices.

CONVERGING CLOSE-HAULED

The diagrams below look at two converging boats on the close-hauled point of sailing. The boat in red is on port tack and is the 'give way' vessel. The green boat is on starboard and is the 'stand on' vessel.

The red boat must avoid the green boat and can do so by steering behind the starboard boat as is shown in the sequence below.

Converging boats sailing close-hauled

The boat on port (red) can turn behind the starboard (green) boat

The boat on port (red) then resumes its close-hauled point of sailing

Alternatively, as shown in the following sequence, the boat on port can tack onto starboard to match the green boat and sail alongside it.

Converging boats sailing close-hauled

The boat on port (red) tack can also tack onto starboard

After tacking, both boats sail parallel to each other

CONVERGING ON OTHER POINTS OF SAILING

The same rule applies if you are sailing with the wind behind you on a broad reach or running point of sailing.

In the following diagrams, once again the boat in red is on port so should avoid the boat in green, which is sailing on starboard.

The red boat has the choice of turning behind the green boat and then continuing on its original point of sailing.

Converging boats sailing on broad reaches

The boat on port (red) can turn behind the starboard (green) boat

The boat on port (red) then resumes its original course

An alternative course of action is again possible for the port boat. Here the boat sailing on port can gybe onto starboard to sail parallel to the green boat.

Converging boats sailing on broad reaches

The boat on port (red) can also gybe onto starboard

After gybing both boats will sail parallel to each other

CLOSE-HAULED VERSUS RUNNING

Another common rule is when two boats converge on different points of sailing.

The diagrams below show a boat sailing close-hauled meeting a boat sailing on a downwind point of sailing. The red boat is close-hauled and sailing on port tack. The green boat is running and on starboard. As before, the red boat must keep out of the way of the green boat.

The best way is to tack onto starboard to sail clear, as is shown in the diagrams below.

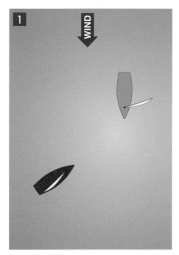

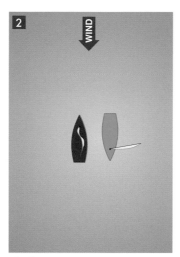

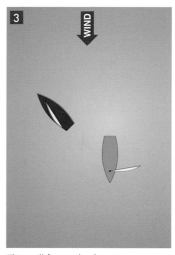

Converging boats – one (red) is sailing on port close-hauled, the other (green) is sailing on a starboard run

The boat on port (red) can avoid the starboard (green) boat by tacking through the wind

This will force the boats on different courses and keep them clear

The alternative is that the red boat sailing on port could push slightly into the no-go zone to slow down in order to let the green boat pass and then steer behind the green boat.

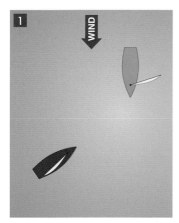

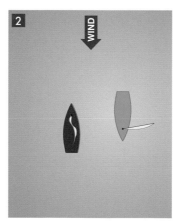

Converging boats – one (red) is sailing on port close-hauled, the other (green) is sailing on a starboard run

The boat on port (red) can gently push into the no-go zone to slow down

Once the starboard (green) boat has passed, both boats resume their original point of sailing

Let's look at this scenario with the situation reversed. This time the boat that is on the running point of sailing is on port (red) meeting a boat that is sailing close-hauled on starboard (green). Once again, the port (red) boat must avoid the starboard (green) boat and then continue on its preferred course.

Converging boats – one (green) is sailing on starboard close-hauled, the other (red) is sailing on a port run

The boat on port (red) steers to avoid the boat on starboard (green)

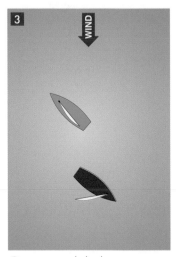

Once passed, the boat on port (red) resumes its original point of sailing

An alternative for the boat running on port (red) is for it to gybe onto starboard and sail clear of the close-hauled boat.

Converging boats – one (green) is sailing on starboard close-hauled, the other (red) is sailing on a port run

The boat on port (red) can gybe to keep clear of the starboard (green) boat

Gybing will keep the boats apart

ON THE SAME TACK
ON DIFFERENT POINTS OF SAILING

Another common situation is when boats converge on different points of sailing but on the same tack. The rules are the same whether both boats are on port tack (as we are illustrating) or on starboard.

The diagrams below show a boat close-hauled on port tack (yellow) sailing directly towards a boat that is on a training run also on port tack (blue). In this situation, it is the boat with the wind behind it (blue) sailing down the page that is the 'give way' vessel, so must take action to avoid the boat sailing up the page (yellow). The boat sailing down the page is often called the windward boat (i.e. the boat that is closest to the wind). When faced with this situation it is the windward boat that should keep clear.

So here, the boat sailing down the page (blue) turns to avoid the boat sailing close-hauled (yellow). Once passed, it resumes its original point of sailing.

Boats converging on the same tack

Windward (blue) boat keeps clear

Windward (blue) steers behind the other boat (yellow)

The alternative (not illustrated) is for the windward boat to gybe onto starboard. The course taken in this situation is similar to the course taken by the windward boat in the previous example (page 184).

ON SIMILAR POINTS OF SAILING

Now let's look at what happens when two boats on the same tack converge that are on very similar points of sailing.

Regardless of the point of sailing they are both on, it is the windward (blue) boat that must keep out of the way.

In our first two examples we have two boats on port on similar converging courses. Here it is the windward (blue) boat that must keep clear and alter its course to avoid a collision with the other (yellow) vessel.

This could be achieved by sailing on a parallel course.

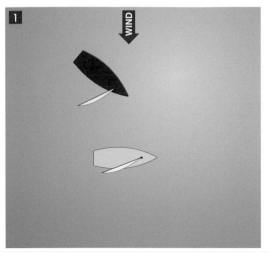

Converging boats on similar points of sailing

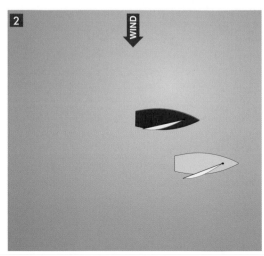

Windward (blue) boat keeps clear and can alter course to match the other (yellow) boat

Alternatively, the windward (blue) boat can alter its course by bearing away from the wind and steering behind the other (yellow) vessel. It can then continue on its original heading.

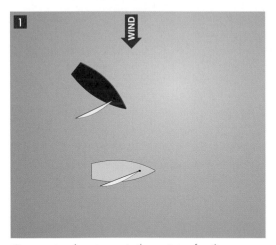

Converging boats on similar points of sailing

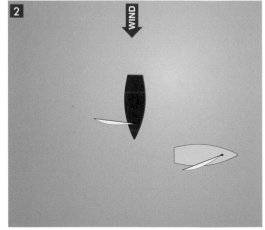

Windward (blue) boat bears away and keeps clear by sailing behind the other (yellow) boat

OVERTAKING

You may also find yourself in a situation where two boats are sailing along exactly the same line on the same point of sailing. In this situation, it is the faster overtaking boat that must keep clear, but it does have choices.

The diagrams opposite illustrate two boats sailing parallel, with the overtaking boat on the left. Here the best course for the overtaking boat is to luff into the wind slightly to take a parallel course to overtake on the windward side. This avoids the disturbed wind pattern under the boom caused by the slower boat. Disturbed wind is called dirty wind or wind shadow and is present under the boom of any boat sailing on the water.

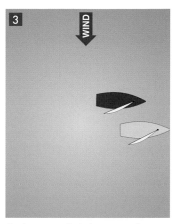

Overtaking (blue) boat keeps clear

Steering to the windward side keeps the overtaking (blue) boat in clear wind

Sailing parallel, the overtaking (blue) boat should pass quickly

Alternatively, the overtaking boat can steer underneath the slower boat and attempt to sail through the wind shadow. But if you do this, it is likely that your ability to overtake will be hindered by the 'dirty' air.

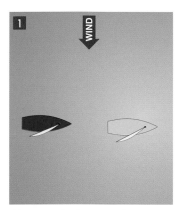

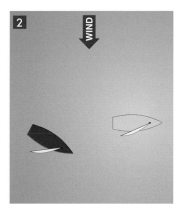

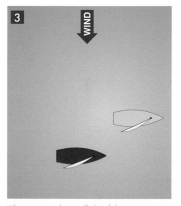

Alternatively the overtaking (blue) boat can pass on the leeward side

The overtaking (blue) boat bears away slightly to keep clear

The overtaking (blue) boat attempts to pass slower boat under its wind shadow

As mentioned, the rules we have shown in this chapter are the most basic so please be aware that additional rules do exist – if in doubt, keep clear of other vessels to avoid collisions well in advance.

KEY LEARNING POINTS

- Keep a good lookout at all times
- Avoid a collision, even if you are the 'stand on' vessel
- Power gives way to sail, with the exception of large commercial and fishing vessels
- Port gives way to starboard
- Windward boat keeps clear of leeward boat
- Overtaking boat keeps clear

GLOSSARY

Aft	At the back of the boat
Ahead	In front of the boat
Astern	Behind the boat
Batten	Lightweight strip inserted into sail to help hold its shape
Beam reach	A point of sailing where the boat is sailing at 90° to the wind
Bearing away	To alter course by turning the boat away from the wind
Beating	Sailing towards the wind in a series of tacks
Boom	A horizontal spar attached to the mast that supports the mainsail
Bow	The forward end of a boat
Bowsprit	A spar that extends from the bow to support the asymmetric spinnaker
Broad reach	A point of sailing where the boat is pointing away from the wind at an angle of approx 135° to the wind
Buoyancy tanks	Sealed tanks in the hull of dinghies that contain buoyancy to support the boat
Burgee	Small flag at the masthead which is used to indicate wind direction
Centreboard	A large plate that pivots and retracts inside the boat, used to prevent sideways slip (called leeway) particularly when sailing close-hauled
Centreline	The centre of the boat running from the stern to the bow
Cleat	Fittings that come in a variety of shapes and sizes either on a boat or pontoon used to secure or hold fast a control or mooring line
Clew	The lower aft corner of a sail
Close-hauled	The point of sailing required to sail as close as possible to the wind. This is the edge of the no-go zone
Close reach	Point of sailing where the boat is approximately 60° to the wind
Cockpit	Recessed area in the boat where the sailors sit
Control line	Piece of rope or cord used to control an individual part of the sail
Crew	The crew is the person controlling the headsail on a two-handed dinghy
Cross-shore wind	Wind that blows parallel to the beach or pontoon
Cunningham	A control line used to tension the luff (leading edge) of the mainsail mainly used on windy days
Daggerboard	Lifting blade that moves up and down through its case to prevent sideways slip (called leeway) particularly when sailing close-hauled
Dagger grip	Term used to describe way that the helmsman holds the mainsheet and tiller extension
Dead run	Point of sailing where the boat is sailing with the wind directly behind
Downhaul	Control line used to either tension the leading edge or luff of the sail. Similar to a cunningham
Drainage bungs	Small close-fitting plugs inserted into drainage ports on the buoyancy tanks
Fairlead	A fixed and rigid fitting normally screwed to the hull that allows a control line to have its direction of travel altered
Foot	Bottom edge of a sail
Fore	Towards the front or bow of the boat
Forestay	A wire rigging that supports the mast at the bow of the boat
Furl	Roll up a sail while still rigged
Gooseneck	Universal joint that connects the boom to the mast

Gudgeon	Fitting on the transom to which the rudder pintle attaches to
Gunwale	The outer edge of the side of a boat
Gybe (gybing)	To change course from one side of the wind to the other, sailing downwind
Halyard	A line either made of rope or wire used to raise sails on a boat, for example 'the main halyard' is the line used to raise the mainsail
Head	Top corner of any sail
Headsail (or jib)	The front sail on a two-handed dinghy controlled by the crew
Head to wind	Position of the boat when the bow is pointing directly into the wind
Helm	The rudder assembly
Helmsman/Helm	Person steering the boat, applies to both male and female
Hove-to	Position where the boat is stopped with the jib or headsail backed and the mainsail flapping
Hull	Main part of the boat
Jam cleat	A cleat which is designed to allow a rope to be fastened quickly
Jib (or headsail)	The front sail on a two-handed dinghy controlled by the crew
Jibsheet	The control line used to pull the jib in or let it out
Kicking strap/ vang	Light tackle angled from the boom to a lower part of the mast or some point on the floor of the boat to stop the boom from rising when the mainsheet is released
Lee	The side facing away from the direction the wind is travelling
Leech	Back edge of a sail
Lee shore	Beach where wind is blowing directly onto it
Leeward	The side of the boat or pontoon opposite to where the wind is blowing from
Luff	The leading edge of a sail
Luff up (luffing)	To turn the boat from one point of sailing to another that is closer to the wind
Lying to	Where the boat is lying on a beam reach point of sailing with the sails released and flapping and the centreboard half raised
Mainsail	The main sail on a boat, the largest sail (except for the spinnaker) controlled by the helmsman
Mainsheet	The line used to pull the mainsail in or let it out
Mainsheet falls	Mainsheet rope and pulley system
Mast	A vertical spar or pole that holds the sails in position
Masthead	The top of a mast
No-go zone	The area in which a boat won't sail, 45° either side of where the wind is blowing from
Offshore wind	A wind blowing off the land
Onshore wind	A wind blowing onto the land, often creates a lee shore
Outhaul	A control line that is used to pull the clew of the sail towards the end of the boom
Painter	A line attached to the bow of dinghies or other small boats for use in securing or mooring
Pintle	Fitting on the rudder head which attaches to the gudgeon on the stern
Planing	When a boat travels fast on a windy day the bow lifts out the water
Point of sailing	Any direction of sailing
Pontoon	A low flat floating platform
Port side	The left side of the boat when looking forwards
Port tack	Any point of sailing with the wind on the left-hand side
Reaching	Holding a course with the wind roughly abeam (on the side of the boat) i.e. sailing across the wind
Reef	Reduce the area of a sail

Reefing	An action that is designed to reduce the size of a sail during periods of strong wind, in order to improve the ship's stability
Retrieval line	Line used to retrieve or stow a sail
Road trailer	Wheeled device that is towed behind a car to transport the boat
Rig	The arrangement of all sails, spars and masts on a boat
Rigging	The system of all ropes, lines and wires that support and control sails and mast on a boat. Also the process of attaching the sails to the boat
Rudder/ rudder blade	A flat, underwater blade that steers the boat
Running	Point of sailing where the wind is behind the boat
Safety pin/clip	Pin designed to secure a removable part of the boat's fixtures or fittings (e.g. rudder)
Self bailer	Through-hull fitting that allows water to drain out of the cockpit when the boat is moving forwards
Shackle	U shaped removable fixing with a pin
Sheet	A control line used to trim sails
Shroud	Wires supporting the mast on either side of the boat
Side tanks	Generally the area that you sit on while sailing, usually the buoyancy tanks
Spar	General term for mast, boom, bowsprit and spinnaker pole
Spinnaker	A large, often colourful sail made of a lightweight cloth
Spinnaker chute	Storage place for the spinnaker when not hoisted
Spreaders	Horizontal brackets fitted to mast to support shrouds
Starboard side	The right side of the boat when looking forwards
Starboard tack	Any point of sailing with the wind on the right-hand side
Stern (or transom)	The back of the boat
Stuck in irons	A term used when the boat is stuck with the bow head to wind
Tack (tacking)	The manoeuvre used to alter direction by turning across the wind, the bow goes from one side of the no-go zone to the other. Or the lower front corner of a sail
Telltales	Strips of fabric attached to sails that are to indicate the wind and right trim
Thwart	Seat running across a dinghy
Tiller	Attachment to the rudder by which it is controlled
Tiller extension	Connected to the tiller, held by the helmsman
Toestraps	Permanently fixed webbing straps to allow helm and crew to lean out
Training run	Point of sailing where the boat is travelling at 150° to the wind
Transom (or stern)	The back end of the boat
Trolley	Wheeled device on which the boat sits on land and is used for launching the boat
Uphaul	A control line used to raise something
Vang/ kicking strap	Light tackle angled from the boom to a lower part of the mast or some point on the floor of the boat to stop the boom from rising when the mainsheet is released
Wearing round	Manoeuvre used to avoid a gybe by tacking but continue sailing on a downwind point of sailing
Windward	Towards the wind

ACKNOWLEDGEMENTS

This book has been created using content from our sailaboattv YouTube channel and is a collaborative effort of lots of people. I would like to thank the partners of Sailaboat Penny King and Nigel Palmer for their drive and vision to get the project off the ground in the first place.

Thanks also to my wife Fay for her enthusiasm and encouragement for all the times I was busy writing, filming and editing.

For the images in the book, thanks go to Tash Jones of Tympani Productions and Simon Vacher for his graphic design.

Thanks also to Evette Tyler Hore for some of the still images.

Thanks to the Laser Centre in Portland for hosting us for the filming period and in particular Hannah Burywood and Pete Ollerenshaw for being such good sports and putting up with days of filming for the video, it is them who you see in most of the pictures.

Thanks also to Littleton Sailing Club who accommodated us for some of the filming and to Laura Glover and Phil Lewis who also appear mainly in the spinnaker chapter.

Also thanks to the club members at Littleton and at Stokes Bay for being photographed.

Thanks to the team at Fernhurst Books for their input and also to Daniel Stephen for the layout.

I would finally like to thank my parents Liz and John for introducing me to the wonderful sport of sailing all those years ago and for encouraging me as a photographer.

Above all thanks to you for buying the book and I really hope that it helps you to learn how to sail.

SAILABOATTV YOUTUBE CHANNEL

SailboatTV's Youtube channel features 109 seperate videos showing you all the aspects of learning to sail as as featured in this book. They are a great supplement to what is shown in this book.